Anonymus

Irish Land Commission Report

August 1889-90

Anonymus

Irish Land Commission Report
August 1889-90

ISBN/EAN: 9783741199882

Manufactured in Europe, USA, Canada, Australia, Japa

Cover: Foto ©Suzi / pixelio.de

Manufactured and distributed by brebook publishing software
(www.brebook.com)

Anonymus

Irish Land Commission Report

IRISH LAND COMMISSION.

[44 & 45 VICT., CH. 49, AND 48 & 49 VICT., CH. 73; 51 & 52 VICT., CH. 38; 52 & 53 VICT., CH. 67; AND 53 & 54 VICT., CH. 12.]

REPORT

OF

THE IRISH LAND COMMISSIONERS

FOR THE PERIOD

FROM 22ND AUGUST, 1889, TO 22ND AUGUST, 1890.

Presented to both Houses of Parliament by Command of Her Majesty.

DUBLIN:
PRINTED FOR HER MAJESTY'S STATIONERY OFFICE,
BY
ALEXANDER THOM & CO. (LIMITED),
And to be purchased, either directly or through any Bookseller, from
EYRE and SPOTTISWOODE, East Harding-street, Fetter-lane, E.C., or 32, Abingdon-street, Westminster, S.W.; or ADAM and CHARLES BLACK, 6, North Bridge, Edinburgh; or
HODGES, FIGGIS, and Co., 104, Grafton-street, Dublin.

INDEX.

INDEX.

Applications for Sale of Tenancies, *Land Law (Ireland) Act*, 1881, section 11.

Total Effect of the Land Law (Ireland) Acts, 1881 & 1887, on the Rental of Ireland.

Applications to Declare Leases Void, *Land Law (Ireland) Act*, 1881, section 21.

Land Sales, *Land Law (Ireland) Act*, 1881, sections 24 to 29, and 34 to 36.

Land Sales, *Purchase of Land (Ireland) Act*, 1885.

Court of the Land Commission Sitting in Dublin.

Labourers' (Ireland) Acts, 1883 to 1886.

Applications to Set Aside Leases on Grounds, *Land Law (Ireland) Act*, 1887, sec. 8.

Leaseholders admitted to Present Tenancy, *Land Law (Ireland) Act*, 1887, sec. 1.

Suspension of Evictions by Instalments, *Land Law (Ireland) Act*, 1887, sec. 8.

Church Temporalities, 44 and 45 *Victoria*, c. 71.

Arrears of Rent (Ireland) Act, 1882.

Collection of Agricultural Prices.

REPORT

OF THE

IRISH LAND COMMISSIONERS

FOR

THE PERIOD BETWEEN THE 21st OF AUGUST, 1889, AND THE 22nd OF AUGUST, 1890.

TO HIS EXCELLENCY LAURENCE DUNDAS, EARL OF ZETLAND,

LORD LIEUTENANT-GENERAL AND GENERAL GOVERNOR OF IRELAND.

PART I.

Report of Commissioners appointed under the Land Law Act of 1881.

We, the Commissioners appointed under the provisions of the Land Law (Ireland) Act, 1881, beg to submit to your Excellency this Report of our proceedings during the twelve months ended on the 21st of August, 1890.

The seven years for which the Land Commission was constituted terminated on the 21st August, 1888. The Commission has, however, been three times continued by the Expiring Laws Continuance Acts of 1888, 1889, and 1890, by the latter of which it has been continued to the 31st December, 1891. Term of Commission.

During the period under review the staff of Assistant Commissioners consisted of 8 legal and 64 lay Commissioners, each legal Assistant Commissioner having four pairs of lay Commissioners associated with him, and sitting in court as chairman successively with one of these pairs. The farms were inspected by the two lay Assistant Commissioners by whom the evidence respecting them was heard. Sub-Commissions.

We have continued to find that the attention and time of the Sub-Commissions have been to a greater extent occupied in dealing with questions of value rather than with questions of law.

The number of fair rent notices disposed of by the Sub-Commissions during the year was 22,972. Of this number 15,095 were cases of applications by yearly tenants, and 7,877 were applications by leaseholders. Originating notices.

The entire number of Fair Rent Notices disposed of during the year was as follows:—

By the Commissioners as Courts of first instance, principally on consent,	1,444
By the Sub-Commissions,	22,972
By the Civil Bill Courts,	4,041
Total,	28,457

The entire number disposed of, by both Land Commission and Civil Bill Courts, from the date of the passing of the Land Law (Ireland) Act, 1881, to the 22nd August, 1890, was 196,762.

The number of Fair Rent Notices awaiting trial by the Land Commission on the 22nd August, 1890, was 43,877, and by the Civil Bill Courts 4,169.

The numbers similarly awaiting trial on the 22nd August, 1890, were :—

By the Land Commission, ...	24,425
By the Civil Bill Courts, ...	4,208

Rents fixed by Court Valuers, by arbitration, and by agreements.

Judicial Rents have been settled during the year by Court Valuers in 132 cases, by Arbitration in 1 case, and by originating declaration and agreement, under the provisions of the 8th section of Land Law (Ireland) Act, 1881, in 5,679 cases, of which 5,506 were filed in the Land Commission and 173 were lodged with the Clerks of the Peace of the Civil Bill Courts, 2 Judicial Leases were executed and 2 Fixed Tenancies created, making altogether 5,816 cases which were settled during the year without litigation.

The total number of rents fixed by originating declaration and agreement, since the passing of the Act of 1881 up to the 22nd August, 1890, was 112,673.

The total number of rents fixed by Court Valuers during the same period was 1,194.

The total number fixed by Arbitration was 37, and of Judicial Leases executed 120 and the number of Fixed Tenancies sanctioned was 28.

Arbitration.

Upon the subject of arbitration, it is to be observed that by the 40th section of the Land Act of 1881 provision was made that if the parties so agree the amount of the judicial rent may be decided by arbitration conducted by arbitrators (one to be appointed by each party), who should name an umpire before the commencement of the arbitration. The power so given has, during the nine years that the Act has been in operation, been availed of in 37 cases, and in only 1 case during the current year.

Leaseholders.

During the year ending 22nd August, 1890, the number of Leaseholders who applied, under the provisions of the Land Law (Ireland) Act, 1887, to the Court of the Land Commission was 1,249, and to the Civil Bill Courts was 1,151.

By the 53 & 54 Vic., cap. 49, the period during which the Civil Bill Courts and the Land Commission were authorised to receive applications from Leaseholders has been extended to the 31st December, 1891.

Total rents fixed.

The entire number of rents fixed by all the methods enumerated from the passing of the Land Law Act in 1881, to the 22nd August, 1890, was 258,784, not including Judicial Leases and Fixed Tenancies. The number of cases struck out, withdrawn, or dismissed was 50,730.

The total number of cases disposed of during the period under review, i.e., from 1881 to 22nd August, 1890, was therefore 309,642.

Appeals.

2,281 Appeals from the Civil Bill Courts and rehearings from the decisions of the Sub-Commissions were disposed of during the year by us, at sittings held on alternate weeks throughout the country, from November to August inclusive. We sat in the intervening weeks during the same period for Appeals from the Dublin District. Sittings were also held in Dublin for the disposal of motions and other court business.

The total number of Appeals disposed of since the passing of the Act in 1881 to the 22nd August, 1890, was 28,816.

The number of Appeals lodged or reinstated during the year was 2,761.

The total number of Appeals pending on the 22nd August, 1890, was 6,412.

Since the date of our last report the requisite assent of Her Majesty's Treasury has been obtained to a rule requiring payment of 10s., stamp duty, upon every Notice of Appeal lodged after the 1st day of February, 1890, where the annual rent of the holding, prior to the date of the order appealed from, exceeds the sum of £10.

While desirous of discouraging unsubstantial appeals we have taken further measures to provide that the Court should be placed in a position to have the best and fullest information before it with reference to such appeals as come before us for decision.

Valuers' reports.

We have therefore instituted the practice of obtaining from one of our Court Valuers, before the date of the hearing, a special report upon the holding, the subject of the Appeal.

When this has been returned to us we cause a notification of the result of such investigation to be immediately sent to the appellant, and either party, if they so desire, can obtain a full copy of the Valuer's Report, upon the subject-matter in question.

We are assured that the information so afforded to the parties is of great assistance. 3,400 copies Reports of Assistant Commissioners and Valuers have been taken out during the year.

The total rental dealt with under the Acts of 1881 and 1887, during the nine years ending 22nd August last, was £5,251,876. The aggregate judicial rent fixed in respect thereof was £4,169,850, amounting to a reduction of 20·6 per cent., over the entire country. Total rents dealt with.

The total rental dealt with during the year under review was £670,115.

Particulars are given by counties in Table XLVII.

During the year orders were sealed under the Labourers Acts, fixing rent in 891 cases of applications from Boards of Guardians, 1 order fixing rent was made by Assistant Commissioners, and 643 such orders have been made by one of the Commissioners, sitting in Chamber in Dublin. The total number of such rents fixed up to 22nd August, 1890, was 2,281. Labourers' Acts.

In Appendix LXIII. particulars are given by counties of the number of such applications received and disposed of, and the average rent payable in respect of these cottage allotments.

Special orders were made in 8 cases by the Sub-Commissions for the erection or improvement of labourers' cottages, under the 19th section of the Land Law (Ireland) Act, 1881, making the total number of such orders 846, to the 22nd August, 1890.

In addition to the orders under the Labourers Acts, and to the orders made on appeal, there were 2,247 orders made in Court, either on notice or *ex-parte* during the year.

The following return shews the number of copies of documents issued during the year from the Office of the Keeper of Records:—

Copies of Orders fixing Judicial Rents, ...	13,858
Copies of Reports of Assistant Commissioners and Valuers, .	3,400
Certificates and Copy of Agreements fixing Judicial Rents, .	5,519
Number of folios of other miscellaneous documents, . . .	15,418

The amount received from the public for scrivenery and other fees during the year amounted to £1,287.

15 applications to set aside leases or grants under section 2 of the Act of 1887 were disposed of during the year.

On the 7th January, 1890, we issued the order and schedule for the temporary adjustment of judicial rents pursuant to the provisions of the 29th section of the Land Law (Ireland) Act, 1887. The schedule annexed to the order was prepared from the returns of prices affecting agricultural produce for the year ended 31st December, 1889. Temporary adjustment of Judicial Rents.

The power conferred on the Land Commission by the provision referred to expired upon the issue of this order.

With the sanction of the Lords Commissioners of Her Majesty's Treasury, we have continued to collect returns of prices of agricultural produce and of live stock from reports furnished to us of sales which actually take place. From these returns the average prices are compiled for each province, and for the whole of Ireland collectively and we publish for the benefit and information of the public quarterly returns of the average price of each of the principal products ascertained in the above manner. We also publish weekly returns of live weight prices obtained in the Dublin, Belfast, and Cork markets. Collection of prices of agricultural produce.

We consider the collection of the returns referred to, representing the actual prices paid for agricultural commodities throughout the country at the principal fairs and other centres as being of great importance. In Appendices LXXVIII., LXXIX., and LXXX., Specimens of the Returns so collected and which have been already published will be found.

The property of the late Established Church, which was vested in us by the 44 & 45 Vic., cap. 71, has been administered by us during the year.

By payments made by us, since the property vested, the total liability has been decreased from £10,481,868 to £7,760,744.

The original debt of £9,000,000, incurred for the purposes of the Church Act, and due to the Commissioners for the Reduction of the National Debt, has been reduced to £8,043,098; at the date of our last Report the amount due was £8,437,087.

Progress has been made in the investigation of liability of lands to tithe-rentcharge; 123 parishes, containing 1,080,188 acres, and subject to £23,008 annual rentcharge payable by 1,903 persons have been investigated and mapped during the past year.

In all, 808 parishes, containing 8,279,879 acres, and subject to £147,923 annual tithe-rentcharge, payable by 14,704 persons have been investigated.

As your Excellency is aware Mr. Justice O'Hagan retired, on account of ill health, from the Judicial Commissionership of this Commission in December, 1889.

(Signed), FREDK. WRENCH.
GERALD FITZGERALD.

JOHN H. FRANKS, Secretary,
31 *October*, 1890.
24, UPPER MERRION-STREET,
Dublin.

PART II.

Report of Commissioners appointed under the Purchase of Land (Ireland) Act, 1885.

We the Commissioners appointed under the provisions of the "Purchase of Land (Ireland) Act, 1885," beg to submit to Your Excellency our fifth Annual Report.

During the five years terminating 21st August, 1890, we received 23,348 applications for advances amounting to £9,217,388, of which 6,813 applications for £1,392,053 were received during the year just closed. Of the above 23,348 applications, 3,303 applications for £1,359,067 were rejected by us on the ground of insufficiency of security or for other reasons. In 1,064 of these cases, in which £507,894 had been first applied for, we subsequently sanctioned advances to the amount of £424,355, leaving the sum of £964,703 as representing applications rejected at the close of the five years. Deducting this amount from the total amount applied for, there would remain out of the sum of £10,000,000 granted for the purposes of the Act an apparent balance on the 21st August, 1890, of £1,747,314 available for future applications. We, however, anticipate that many of the more recent applications refused by us will be renewed upon the basis of reduced advances. *Applications received. Cases refused. State of grant.*

The 23,348 applications were made in respect of holdings upon the estates of 1,519 different landlords, 384 of these estates being in Ulster, 526 in Munster, 443 in Leinster, and 159 in Connaught. *Classification as to estates.*

The following table shows the number of applications received and the advances applied for during each of the five years covered by this report.

Provinces.	[illegible]		[illegible]		[illegible]		[illegible]		[illegible]		Total.	
	No.	Amount.	No.	Amount.	No.	Amount.	No.	Amount.	No.	Amount.	No.	Amount.
		£		£		£		£		£		£
Ulster	[illegible]	[illegible]	[illegible]	[illegible]	[illegible]	[illegible]	[illegible]	[illegible]	[illegible]	[illegible]	[illegible]	[illegible]
Munster	[illegible]	[illegible]	[illegible]	[illegible]	[illegible]	[illegible]	[illegible]	[illegible]	[illegible]	[illegible]	[illegible]	[illegible]
Leinster	[illegible]	[illegible]	[illegible]	[illegible]	[illegible]	[illegible]	[illegible]	[illegible]	[illegible]	[illegible]	[illegible]	[illegible]
Connaught	[illegible]	[illegible]	[illegible]	[illegible]	[illegible]	[illegible]	[illegible]	[illegible]	[illegible]	[illegible]	[illegible]	[illegible]
Total	[illegible]	[illegible]	[illegible]	[illegible]	[illegible]	[illegible]	[illegible]	[illegible]	[illegible]	[illegible]	[illegible]	[illegible]

Of the 6,813 applications received during the year 1890, there were, in respect of holdings— *Classification of holdings.*

Not exceeding 1 Acre.	[illegible]	[illegible]	[illegible]	[illegible]	[illegible]	[illegible]	[illegible]	[illegible]	Exceeding 200 Acres.
358	531	871	463	566	585	433	221	47	23

We have provisionally sanctioned 17,650 applications for £7,807,118, of which 3,531 applications for £1,434,188 were sanctioned during the year just closed, while 3,559 applications for £943,673 were at the close of the year under investigation, or awaiting the results of surveys or other preliminary inquiries, and are now being ruled. *Loans sanctioned.*

Of the 17,550 applications for £7,807,113 so sanctioned by us, we have issued 13,721 loans amounting to £5,758,237, including the sum of £160,477 advanced upon thirty-five estates bought by us in the Land Judges' Court, under the 5th Section of the Act for re-sale to the tenants. The amount issued during the year was £1,128,382. The proceedings towards the issue of the sum of £1,548,876 (being the difference between the amount sanctioned and the amount paid) are now in progress. *Loans issued. Purchase of estates.*

Of the 13,721 loans issued, amounting to £5,758,187—7,214, amounting to £2,119,976, were for Ulster; 2,979, amounting to £1,875,812, were for Munster; 2,246, amounting to £1,403,952, were for Leinster; and 1,388, amounting to £355,486, were for Connaught. *Distribution of purchase-money in Provinces.*

Classification of purchases.

Of these 18,731 Loans issued—

1,020	were for sums not exceeding		£50,	the amount advanced being	£36,[illegible]
2,146	were for sums exceeding	£50 and not exceeding	£100,	"	[illegible]
3,329	"	" £100	£300,	"	[illegible]
4,068	"	" £300	£500,	"	[illegible]
1,071	"	" £500	£700,	"	[illegible]
780	"	" £700	£1,000,	"	[illegible]
585	"	" £1,000	£1,500,	"	[illegible]
321	"	" £1,500	£2,000,	"	[illegible]
196	"	" £2,000	£3,000,	"	[illegible]
30	"	" £3,000	£4,000,	"	[illegible]
48	"	" £4,000	£5,000,	"	[illegible]

Payment in cash by purchasers. Guarantee Deposits.

In 193 of these cases the purchase money in excess of the advances was provided by cash payments amounting to £71,735, and by mortgages to the amount of £26,315. In 98 cases the tenants lodged in cash the Guarantee Deposits, the sums so lodged being £24,438. The total amount of Guarantee Deposits lodged or retained was £1,141,173, of which £188,959 has been invested upon the application of the parties interested therein, in securities as authorized by the Act of 1887.

Average rates of purchase agreed upon.

In the cases in which advances have been provisionally sanctioned during the five years, the average prices for all Ireland, calculated upon the rents, were, in 1886, 18 times the rent; in 1887, 17·6; in 1888, 17·0; in 1889, 16·4, and in 1890, 16·7.

Taken in counties, the averages during the five years ranged in 1886 from 23·8 to 13·8; in 1887 from 20·6 to 11·5; in 1888 from 19·7 to 12·4; in 1889 from 19·7 to 13·2, and in 1890 from 19·8 to 13·2. In our last annual report we called attention to some of the disturbing elements which an analysis of the details of the circumstances of the cases dealt with would disclose, and which render these tables of averages unreliable as indicating the selling value of any particular estate or holding, and they cannot be regarded as being capable of general application.

Repayment of advances.

The collection of instalments in repayment of advances under the Purchase of Land Act, 1885 (which, as your Excellency is aware, is made by means of remittable orders issued by post from our Collection Department, and without the intervention of local or other agents), continues to be satisfactory.

The number of payers under that Act on the books of the Land Commission on the 1st of May, 1890, was 11,878, as against 8,670 at the corresponding date in 1889. The total amount receivable in respect of interest and instalments from the date of the passing of the Act to the 1st May, 1890, was £409,598, of which sum £184,236 have accrued during the year just ended. The total amount of arrears unpaid on the 21st August, 1890, was £7,657, which, up to the 31st of October, has been reduced to £2,554, due from 258 payers. With the exception of £611 the entire of this arrear is due in respect of the half-yearly instalments of £99,246 which became payable on the 1st May, 1890.

This arrear of £2,554 is equal to ⅝ per centum of the total amount receivable as against an arrear of 1½ per centum of the total amount receivable on the same date last year, or if the comparison be limited to the half-yearly instalments which accrued due on 1st May, 1889, and on 1st May, 1890, it will be found that the existing arrear represents less than 2 per centum of the half-yearly amount in collection as against an arrear of 8½ per centum of the collection in 1889.

Having regard to the large number of payers on our books, many of whom were in the habit of paying their rents annually, or at uncertain periods, the character of the holdings sold, and the varying circumstances of the purchasers, these results are evidence of the creditable regularity with which the majority of the purchasers have discharged their new engagements. When, however, default is made in the payment of a half-yearly instalment, after sufficient notice, proceedings are instituted, either by action or civil bill process, against the debtor, as directed by the 18th section of the Act of 1887, and every effort is made to recover the amount due before resorting to a sale of the holding. In almost all cases of default we have found that the claims have been met upon the institution of proceedings.

During the five years ending 21st August, 1890, the holdings of twenty-seven defaulters were put for sale; thirteen of these holdings were sold to ordinary purchasers; eleven holdings, for which there was no competition, were purchased by the former landlords. In these cases the holdings were sold subject to the future payment of the annuities, the amounts realised being applied towards the discharge of the arrears due at the time of sale. In three cases, in which there were no bidders, the holdings are in the hands of the Land Commission pending re-sale.

During the five years covered by this report the Guarantee Deposits in the cases of seven holdings were applied by us to the discharge of unpaid instalments, and up to the present time no loss to the State has occurred in respect of any advances made under the Act.

During the five years under review, 1,519 Abstracts of Title were lodged, and in all these cases, with the exception of 48, the rulings have been issued. The drafts of 2,671 Vesting Orders or Conveyances were settled during the year, the total number settled during the five years being 13,671. Since the passing of the Act of 1887, we have availed ourselves as far as possible of the provisions of that Act in relation to the redemption of Head Rents and other annual outgoings, with the result that in the majority of the cases recently closed the sales have been effected discharged of outgoings, and in 97 estates we have ordered the redemption or apportionment and redemption of Head Rents. Without reference to the legal questions that have arisen in the earlier stages of the proceedings towards the sales now in progress, we have exercised the legal jurisdiction conferred upon us by statute in respect of the questions arising in the proceedings for the sale of 835 different estates, and the distribution of nearly £6,000,000, the proceeds of such sales. Since the passing of the Act of 1885 seventeen questions of law were heard and determined by the Judicial Commissioner sitting with us, in pursuance of the 17th section of that Act. The number of appeals to the Court of Appeal were three. In the year just closed £458,432 were lodged in the Bank of Ireland, under the provisions of the 14th section of the Act of 1887, for expediting sales; and as suitors now appreciate the advantage of carrying out their proceedings by means of Vesting Orders, we anticipate that a very large number of the loans which have been provisionally sanctioned will have been issued during the early part of the coming year. Progress of business.

(Signed), E. J. LYNCH.
JOHN GEORGE MACCARTHY.

JOHN H. FRANKS, Secretary,

21st October, 1890.

24, Upper Merrion Street, Dublin.

APPENDIX.

Fair Rent Returns—Tables I. to XIV. inclusive.

Section 8, Sub-section 1.—Land Law (Ireland) Act, 1881.

Section 1.—Land Law (Ireland) Act, 1887.

I.—Table showing, according to Provinces and Counties, the Number of Originating Notices to fix Fair Rents lodged with the Irish Land Commission, the Number of such Notices transferred from the Civil Bill Courts to the Irish Land Commission, the Number of Rents fixed by Chief Commission, Sub-Commissions, and Valuers, and of Cases Dismissed, Struck out, and Withdrawn during the year ended 21st August, 1890.

Province and County.	Number of Originating Notices to fix Fair Rents lodged.		Notices transferred from Civil Bill Courts.		Total Number of Cases.	Number of Rents fixed.					Rents fixed by Valuers.	Number of Applications Dismissed, Struck out, and Withdrawn.	Total Number of Cases disposed of.
						By Chief Commission.			By Sub-Commissions.				
	Yearly Tenancies.	Leasehold Tenancies.	Yearly Tenancies.	Leasehold Tenancies.		Yearly Tenancies.	Leasehold Tenancies.	By Agreement.	Yearly Tenancies.	Leasehold Tenancies.			
Ulster:													
Antrim,	[illegible]	[illegible]	[illegible]	[illegible]	[illegible]	[illegible]	[illegible]	[illegible]	[illegible]	[illegible]	[illegible]	[illegible]	[illegible]
Armagh,	[illegible]	[illegible]	[illegible]	[illegible]	[illegible]	[illegible]	[illegible]	[illegible]	[illegible]	[illegible]	[illegible]	[illegible]	[illegible]
Cavan,	[illegible]	[illegible]	[illegible]	[illegible]	[illegible]	[illegible]	[illegible]	[illegible]	[illegible]	[illegible]	[illegible]	[illegible]	[illegible]
Donegal,	[illegible]	[illegible]	[illegible]	[illegible]	[illegible]	[illegible]	[illegible]	[illegible]	[illegible]	[illegible]	[illegible]	[illegible]	[illegible]
Down,	[illegible]	[illegible]	[illegible]	[illegible]	[illegible]	[illegible]	[illegible]	[illegible]	[illegible]	[illegible]	[illegible]	[illegible]	[illegible]
Fermanagh,	[illegible]	[illegible]	[illegible]	[illegible]	[illegible]	[illegible]	[illegible]	[illegible]	[illegible]	[illegible]	[illegible]	[illegible]	[illegible]
Londonderry,	[illegible]	[illegible]	[illegible]	[illegible]	[illegible]	[illegible]	[illegible]	[illegible]	[illegible]	[illegible]	[illegible]	[illegible]	[illegible]
Monaghan,	[illegible]	[illegible]	[illegible]	[illegible]	[illegible]	[illegible]	[illegible]	[illegible]	[illegible]	[illegible]	[illegible]	[illegible]	[illegible]
Tyrone,	[illegible]	[illegible]	[illegible]	[illegible]	[illegible]	[illegible]	[illegible]	[illegible]	[illegible]	[illegible]	[illegible]	[illegible]	[illegible]
Total,	[illegible]	[illegible]	[illegible]	[illegible]	[illegible]	[illegible]	[illegible]	[illegible]	[illegible]	[illegible]	[illegible]	[illegible]	[illegible]
Leinster:													
Carlow,	[illegible]	[illegible]	[illegible]	[illegible]	[illegible]	[illegible]	[illegible]	[illegible]	[illegible]	[illegible]	[illegible]	[illegible]	[illegible]
Dublin,	[illegible]	[illegible]	[illegible]	[illegible]	[illegible]	[illegible]	[illegible]	[illegible]	[illegible]	[illegible]	[illegible]	[illegible]	[illegible]
Kildare,	[illegible]	[illegible]	[illegible]	[illegible]	[illegible]	[illegible]	[illegible]	[illegible]	[illegible]	[illegible]	[illegible]	[illegible]	[illegible]
Kilkenny,	[illegible]	[illegible]	[illegible]	[illegible]	[illegible]	[illegible]	[illegible]	[illegible]	[illegible]	[illegible]	[illegible]	[illegible]	[illegible]
King's,	[illegible]	[illegible]	[illegible]	[illegible]	[illegible]	[illegible]	[illegible]	[illegible]	[illegible]	[illegible]	[illegible]	[illegible]	[illegible]
Longford,	[illegible]	[illegible]	[illegible]	[illegible]	[illegible]	[illegible]	[illegible]	[illegible]	[illegible]	[illegible]	[illegible]	[illegible]	[illegible]
Louth,	[illegible]	[illegible]	[illegible]	[illegible]	[illegible]	[illegible]	[illegible]	[illegible]	[illegible]	[illegible]	[illegible]	[illegible]	[illegible]
Meath,	[illegible]	[illegible]	[illegible]	[illegible]	[illegible]	[illegible]	[illegible]	[illegible]	[illegible]	[illegible]	[illegible]	[illegible]	[illegible]
Queen's,	[illegible]	[illegible]	[illegible]	[illegible]	[illegible]	[illegible]	[illegible]	[illegible]	[illegible]	[illegible]	[illegible]	[illegible]	[illegible]
Westmeath,	[illegible]	[illegible]	[illegible]	[illegible]	[illegible]	[illegible]	[illegible]	[illegible]	[illegible]	[illegible]	[illegible]	[illegible]	[illegible]
Wexford,	[illegible]	[illegible]	[illegible]	[illegible]	[illegible]	[illegible]	[illegible]	[illegible]	[illegible]	[illegible]	[illegible]	[illegible]	[illegible]
Wicklow,	[illegible]	[illegible]	[illegible]	[illegible]	[illegible]	[illegible]	[illegible]	[illegible]	[illegible]	[illegible]	[illegible]	[illegible]	[illegible]
Total,	[illegible]	[illegible]	[illegible]	[illegible]	[illegible]	[illegible]	[illegible]	[illegible]	[illegible]	[illegible]	[illegible]	[illegible]	[illegible]
Connaught:													
Galway,	[illegible]	[illegible]	[illegible]	[illegible]	[illegible]	[illegible]	[illegible]	[illegible]	[illegible]	[illegible]	[illegible]	[illegible]	[illegible]
Leitrim,	[illegible]	[illegible]	[illegible]	[illegible]	[illegible]	[illegible]	[illegible]	[illegible]	[illegible]	[illegible]	[illegible]	[illegible]	[illegible]
Mayo,	[illegible]	[illegible]	[illegible]	[illegible]	[illegible]	[illegible]	[illegible]	[illegible]	[illegible]	[illegible]	[illegible]	[illegible]	[illegible]
Roscommon,	[illegible]	[illegible]	[illegible]	[illegible]	[illegible]	[illegible]	[illegible]	[illegible]	[illegible]	[illegible]	[illegible]	[illegible]	[illegible]
Sligo,	[illegible]	[illegible]	[illegible]	[illegible]	[illegible]	[illegible]	[illegible]	[illegible]	[illegible]	[illegible]	[illegible]	[illegible]	[illegible]
Total,	[illegible]	[illegible]	[illegible]	[illegible]	[illegible]	[illegible]	[illegible]	[illegible]	[illegible]	[illegible]	[illegible]	[illegible]	[illegible]
Munster:													
Clare,	[illegible]	[illegible]	[illegible]	[illegible]	[illegible]	[illegible]	[illegible]	[illegible]	[illegible]	[illegible]	[illegible]	[illegible]	[illegible]
Cork,	[illegible]	[illegible]	[illegible]	[illegible]	[illegible]	[illegible]	[illegible]	[illegible]	[illegible]	[illegible]	[illegible]	[illegible]	[illegible]
Kerry,	[illegible]	[illegible]	[illegible]	[illegible]	[illegible]	[illegible]	[illegible]	[illegible]	[illegible]	[illegible]	[illegible]	[illegible]	[illegible]
Limerick,	[illegible]	[illegible]	[illegible]	[illegible]	[illegible]	[illegible]	[illegible]	[illegible]	[illegible]	[illegible]	[illegible]	[illegible]	[illegible]
Tipperary,	[illegible]	[illegible]	[illegible]	[illegible]	[illegible]	[illegible]	[illegible]	[illegible]	[illegible]	[illegible]	[illegible]	[illegible]	[illegible]
Waterford,	[illegible]	[illegible]	[illegible]	[illegible]	[illegible]	[illegible]	[illegible]	[illegible]	[illegible]	[illegible]	[illegible]	[illegible]	[illegible]
Total,	[illegible]	[illegible]	[illegible]	[illegible]	[illegible]	[illegible]	[illegible]	[illegible]	[illegible]	[illegible]	[illegible]	[illegible]	[illegible]
SUMMARY:													
Ulster,	[illegible]	[illegible]	[illegible]	[illegible]	[illegible]	[illegible]	[illegible]	[illegible]	[illegible]	[illegible]	[illegible]	[illegible]	[illegible]
Leinster,	[illegible]	[illegible]	[illegible]	[illegible]	[illegible]	[illegible]	[illegible]	[illegible]	[illegible]	[illegible]	[illegible]	[illegible]	[illegible]
Connaught,	[illegible]	[illegible]	[illegible]	[illegible]	[illegible]	[illegible]	[illegible]	[illegible]	[illegible]	[illegible]	[illegible]	[illegible]	[illegible]
Munster,	[illegible]	[illegible]	[illegible]	[illegible]	[illegible]	[illegible]	[illegible]	[illegible]	[illegible]	[illegible]	[illegible]	[illegible]	[illegible]
Total,	[illegible]	[illegible]	[illegible]	[illegible]	[illegible]	[illegible]	[illegible]	[illegible]	[illegible]	[illegible]	[illegible]	[illegible]	[illegible]

II.—TABLE showing, according to Provinces and Counties, the number of Originating Notices to fix Fair Rents lodged with the Irish Land Commission, the number of such Notices transferred from the Civil Bill Courts to the Irish Land Commission, the number of Rents fixed by Chief Commission, Sub-Commissions, and Valuers, and of Cases Dismissed, Struck out, and Withdrawn, during the nine years ended 31st August, 1890.

Provinces and Counties.	Number of Originating Notices to fix Fair Rents lodged.		Number transferred from Civil Bill Courts.		Total Number of Cases.	Number of Rents fixed. By Chief Commission.			By Sub-Commissions.		Total Number of Rents fixed.	Number of applications Dismissed, Struck out, and Withdrawn.	Total Number of cases disposed of.	Number of cases undisposed of.
	[illegible]	[illegible]	[illegible]	[illegible]		[illegible]	[illegible]	[illegible]	[illegible]	[illegible]				
ULSTER:														
Antrim,	[illegible]	[illegible]	[illegible]	-	[illegible]	[illegible]	[illegible]	[illegible]	[illegible]	[illegible]	[illegible]	[illegible]	[illegible]	[illegible]
Armagh,	[illegible]	[illegible]	-	-	[illegible]	[illegible]	[illegible]	-	[illegible]	[illegible]	[illegible]	[illegible]	[illegible]	[illegible]
Cavan,	[illegible]	[illegible]	[illegible]	[illegible]	[illegible]	[illegible]	[illegible]	[illegible]	[illegible]	[illegible]	[illegible]	[illegible]	[illegible]	[illegible]
Donegal,	[illegible]	[illegible]	[illegible]	-	[illegible]	[illegible]	[illegible]	[illegible]	[illegible]	[illegible]	[illegible]	[illegible]	[illegible]	[illegible]
Down,	[illegible]	[illegible]	[illegible]	-	[illegible]	[illegible]	[illegible]	-	[illegible]	[illegible]	[illegible]	[illegible]	[illegible]	[illegible]
Fermanagh,	[illegible]	[illegible]	[illegible]	[illegible]	[illegible]	[illegible]	[illegible]	[illegible]	[illegible]	[illegible]	[illegible]	[illegible]	[illegible]	[illegible]
Londonderry,	[illegible]	[illegible]	[illegible]	[illegible]	[illegible]	[illegible]	[illegible]	-	[illegible]	[illegible]	[illegible]	[illegible]	[illegible]	[illegible]
Monaghan,	[illegible]	[illegible]	[illegible]	-	[illegible]	[illegible]	[illegible]	[illegible]	[illegible]	[illegible]	[illegible]	[illegible]	[illegible]	[illegible]
Tyrone,	[illegible]	[illegible]	[illegible]	[illegible]	[illegible]	[illegible]	[illegible]	[illegible]	[illegible]	[illegible]	[illegible]	[illegible]	[illegible]	[illegible]
Total,	[illegible]	[illegible]	[illegible]	[illegible]	[illegible]	[illegible]	[illegible]	[illegible]	[illegible]	[illegible]	[illegible]	[illegible]	[illegible]	[illegible]
LEINSTER:														
Carlow,	[illegible]	[illegible]	[illegible]	-	[illegible]	[illegible]	[illegible]	[illegible]	[illegible]	[illegible]	[illegible]	[illegible]	[illegible]	[illegible]
Dublin,	[illegible]	[illegible]	[illegible]		[illegible]	[illegible]	[illegible]	[illegible]	[illegible]	[illegible]	[illegible]	[illegible]	[illegible]	[illegible]
Kildare,	[illegible]	[illegible]	[illegible]		[illegible]	[illegible]	[illegible]	[illegible]	[illegible]	[illegible]	[illegible]	[illegible]	[illegible]	[illegible]
Kilkenny,	[illegible]	[illegible]	[illegible]	[illegible]	[illegible]	[illegible]	[illegible]	[illegible]	[illegible]	[illegible]	[illegible]	[illegible]	[illegible]	[illegible]
King's,	[illegible]	[illegible]	[illegible]	[illegible]	[illegible]	[illegible]	[illegible]	[illegible]	[illegible]	[illegible]	[illegible]	[illegible]	[illegible]	[illegible]
Longford,	[illegible]	[illegible]	[illegible]	[illegible]	[illegible]	[illegible]	[illegible]	[illegible]	[illegible]	[illegible]	[illegible]	[illegible]	[illegible]	[illegible]
Louth,	[illegible]	[illegible]	[illegible]	[illegible]	[illegible]	[illegible]	[illegible]	[illegible]	[illegible]	[illegible]	[illegible]	[illegible]	[illegible]	[illegible]
Meath,	[illegible]	[illegible]	[illegible]	[illegible]	[illegible]	[illegible]	[illegible]	[illegible]	[illegible]	[illegible]	[illegible]	[illegible]	[illegible]	[illegible]
Queen's,	[illegible]	[illegible]	[illegible]	[illegible]	[illegible]	[illegible]	[illegible]	[illegible]	[illegible]	[illegible]	[illegible]	[illegible]	[illegible]	[illegible]
Westmeath,	[illegible]	[illegible]	[illegible]	[illegible]	[illegible]	[illegible]	[illegible]	[illegible]	[illegible]	[illegible]	[illegible]	[illegible]	[illegible]	[illegible]
Wexford,	[illegible]	[illegible]	[illegible]	-	[illegible]	[illegible]	[illegible]	[illegible]	[illegible]	[illegible]	[illegible]	[illegible]	[illegible]	[illegible]
Wicklow,	[illegible]	[illegible]	[illegible]	-	[illegible]	[illegible]	[illegible]	[illegible]	[illegible]	[illegible]	[illegible]	[illegible]	[illegible]	[illegible]
Total,	[illegible]	[illegible]	[illegible]	[illegible]	[illegible]	[illegible]	[illegible]	[illegible]	[illegible]	[illegible]	[illegible]	[illegible]	[illegible]	[illegible]
CONNAUGHT:														
Galway,	[illegible]	[illegible]	[illegible]	-	[illegible]	[illegible]	[illegible]	[illegible]	[illegible]	[illegible]	[illegible]	[illegible]	[illegible]	[illegible]
Leitrim,	[illegible]	[illegible]	[illegible]	[illegible]	[illegible]	[illegible]	[illegible]	[illegible]	[illegible]	[illegible]	[illegible]	[illegible]	[illegible]	[illegible]
Mayo,	[illegible]	[illegible]	[illegible]	[illegible]	[illegible]	[illegible]	[illegible]	[illegible]	[illegible]	[illegible]	[illegible]	[illegible]	[illegible]	[illegible]
Roscommon,	[illegible]	[illegible]	[illegible]	-	[illegible]	[illegible]	[illegible]	[illegible]	[illegible]	[illegible]	[illegible]	[illegible]	[illegible]	[illegible]
Sligo,	[illegible]	[illegible]	[illegible]	-	[illegible]	[illegible]	[illegible]	[illegible]	[illegible]	[illegible]	[illegible]	[illegible]	[illegible]	[illegible]
Total,	[illegible]	[illegible]	[illegible]	[illegible]	[illegible]	[illegible]	[illegible]	[illegible]	[illegible]	[illegible]	[illegible]	[illegible]	[illegible]	[illegible]
MUNSTER:														
Clare,	[illegible]	[illegible]	[illegible]	-	[illegible]	[illegible]	[illegible]	[illegible]	[illegible]	[illegible]	[illegible]	[illegible]	[illegible]	[illegible]
Cork,	[illegible]	[illegible]	[illegible]	[illegible]	[illegible]	[illegible]	[illegible]	[illegible]	[illegible]	[illegible]	[illegible]	[illegible]	[illegible]	[illegible]
Kerry,	[illegible]	[illegible]	[illegible]	[illegible]	[illegible]	-	[illegible]	[illegible]	[illegible]	[illegible]	[illegible]	[illegible]	[illegible]	[illegible]
Limerick,	[illegible]	[illegible]	[illegible]	[illegible]	[illegible]	-	[illegible]	[illegible]	[illegible]	[illegible]	[illegible]	[illegible]	[illegible]	[illegible]
Tipperary,	[illegible]	[illegible]	[illegible]	[illegible]	[illegible]	[illegible]	[illegible]	[illegible]	[illegible]	[illegible]	[illegible]	[illegible]	[illegible]	[illegible]
Waterford,	[illegible]	[illegible]	[illegible]	[illegible]	[illegible]	-	[illegible]	[illegible]	[illegible]	[illegible]	[illegible]	[illegible]	[illegible]	[illegible]
Total,	[illegible]	[illegible]	[illegible]	[illegible]	[illegible]	[illegible]	[illegible]	[illegible]	[illegible]	[illegible]	[illegible]	[illegible]	[illegible]	[illegible]
SUMMARY.														
Ulster,	[illegible]	[illegible]	[illegible]	[illegible]	[illegible]	[illegible]	[illegible]	[illegible]	[illegible]	[illegible]	[illegible]	[illegible]	[illegible]	[illegible]
Leinster,	[illegible]	[illegible]	[illegible]	[illegible]	[illegible]	[illegible]	[illegible]	[illegible]	[illegible]	[illegible]	[illegible]	[illegible]	[illegible]	[illegible]
Connaught,	[illegible]	[illegible]	[illegible]	[illegible]	[illegible]	[illegible]	[illegible]	[illegible]	[illegible]	[illegible]	[illegible]	[illegible]	[illegible]	[illegible]
Munster,	[illegible]	[illegible]	[illegible]	[illegible]	[illegible]	[illegible]	[illegible]	[illegible]	[illegible]	[illegible]	[illegible]	[illegible]	[illegible]	[illegible]
Total,	[illegible]	[illegible]	[illegible]	[illegible]	[illegible]	[illegible]	[illegible]	[illegible]	[illegible]	[illegible]	[illegible]	[illegible]	[illegible]	[illegible]

* Some of these Rents may have been fixed in cases where the Court had previously made orders that the Lessees of the holdings be deemed Tenants of present tenancies under Section 1, Land Law (Ireland) Act, 1887. See Table LXIX.

III.—TABLE showing, according to Provinces and Counties, the Number of Cases in which Judicial Rents have been fixed for Yearly Tenancies by Chief Commission and Sub-Commissions during the year ended the 31st August, 1890; and also a Summary of the Acreage, Tenement Valuation, Former Rents, Judicial Rents of the Holdings, and the Per-centage of Reductions made in the Former Rents.

Provinces and Counties.	Number of Cases in which Judicial Rents have been fixed.	Acreage. Statute Acres.	Tenement Valuation.	Former Rent.	Judicial Rent.	Per-centage of Reduction.
		a. r. p.	£ s. d.	£ s. d.	£ s. d.	
ULSTER:						
Antrim,	[illegible]	[illegible]	[illegible]	[illegible]	[illegible]	[illegible]
Armagh,	[illegible]	[illegible]	[illegible]	[illegible]	[illegible]	[illegible]
Cavan,	[illegible]	[illegible]	[illegible]	[illegible]	[illegible]	[illegible]
Donegal,	[illegible]	[illegible]	[illegible]	[illegible]	[illegible]	[illegible]
Down,	[illegible]	[illegible]	[illegible]	[illegible]	[illegible]	[illegible]
Fermanagh,	[illegible]	[illegible]	[illegible]	[illegible]	[illegible]	[illegible]
Londonderry,	[illegible]	[illegible]	[illegible]	[illegible]	[illegible]	[illegible]
Monaghan,	[illegible]	[illegible]	[illegible]	[illegible]	[illegible]	[illegible]
Tyrone,	[illegible]	[illegible]	[illegible]	[illegible]	[illegible]	[illegible]
Total,	[illegible]	[illegible]	[illegible]	[illegible]	[illegible]	[illegible]
LEINSTER:						
Carlow,	[illegible]	[illegible]	[illegible]	[illegible]	[illegible]	[illegible]
Dublin,	[illegible]	[illegible]	[illegible]	[illegible]	[illegible]	[illegible]
Kildare,	[illegible]	[illegible]	[illegible]	[illegible]	[illegible]	[illegible]
Kilkenny,	[illegible]	[illegible]	[illegible]	[illegible]	[illegible]	[illegible]
King's,	[illegible]	[illegible]	[illegible]	[illegible]	[illegible]	[illegible]
Longford,	[illegible]	[illegible]	[illegible]	[illegible]	[illegible]	[illegible]
Louth,	[illegible]	[illegible]	[illegible]	[illegible]	[illegible]	[illegible]
Meath,	[illegible]	[illegible]	[illegible]	[illegible]	[illegible]	[illegible]
Queen's,	[illegible]	[illegible]	[illegible]	[illegible]	[illegible]	[illegible]
Westmeath,	[illegible]	[illegible]	[illegible]	[illegible]	[illegible]	[illegible]
Wexford,	[illegible]	[illegible]	[illegible]	[illegible]	[illegible]	[illegible]
Wicklow,	[illegible]	[illegible]	[illegible]	[illegible]	[illegible]	[illegible]
Total,	[illegible]	[illegible]	[illegible]	[illegible]	[illegible]	[illegible]
CONNAUGHT:						
Galway,	[illegible]	[illegible]	[illegible]	[illegible]	[illegible]	[illegible]
Leitrim,	[illegible]	[illegible]	[illegible]	[illegible]	[illegible]	[illegible]
Mayo,	[illegible]	[illegible]	[illegible]	[illegible]	[illegible]	[illegible]
Roscommon,	[illegible]	[illegible]	[illegible]	[illegible]	[illegible]	[illegible]
Sligo,	[illegible]	[illegible]	[illegible]	[illegible]	[illegible]	[illegible]
Total,	[illegible]	[illegible]	[illegible]	[illegible]	[illegible]	[illegible]
MUNSTER:						
Clare,	[illegible]	[illegible]	[illegible]	[illegible]	[illegible]	[illegible]
Cork,	[illegible]	[illegible]	[illegible]	[illegible]	[illegible]	[illegible]
Kerry,	[illegible]	[illegible]	[illegible]	[illegible]	[illegible]	[illegible]
Limerick,	[illegible]	[illegible]	[illegible]	[illegible]	[illegible]	[illegible]
Tipperary,	[illegible]	[illegible]	[illegible]	[illegible]	[illegible]	[illegible]
Waterford,	[illegible]	[illegible]	[illegible]	[illegible]	[illegible]	[illegible]
Total,	[illegible]	[illegible]	[illegible]	[illegible]	[illegible]	[illegible]
SUMMARY.						
Ulster,	[illegible]	[illegible]	[illegible]	[illegible]	[illegible]	[illegible]
Leinster,	[illegible]	[illegible]	[illegible]	[illegible]	[illegible]	[illegible]
Connaught,	[illegible]	[illegible]	[illegible]	[illegible]	[illegible]	[illegible]
Munster,	[illegible]	[illegible]	[illegible]	[illegible]	[illegible]	[illegible]
Total,	[illegible]	[illegible]	[illegible]	[illegible]	[illegible]	[illegible]

IV.—Table showing, according to Provinces and Counties, the Number of Cases in which Judicial Rents have been fixed for Yearly Tenancies by Chief Commission and Sub-Commissions during the Nine Years ended the 21st August, 1890; and also a Summary of the Acreage, Tenement Valuations, Former Rents, Judicial Rents of the Holdings, and the Percentages of Reductions made in the Former Rents.

Provinces and Counties.	Number of Cases in which Judicial Rents have been fixed.	Acreage, Statute Acres.	Tenement Valuation.	Former Rent.	Judicial Rent.	Percentage of Reduction.
		A. R. P.	£ s. d.	£ s. d.	£ s. d.	
Ulster:						
Antrim,	[illegible]	[illegible]	[illegible]	[illegible]	[illegible]	[illegible]
Armagh,	[illegible]	[illegible]	[illegible]	[illegible]	[illegible]	[illegible]
Cavan,	[illegible]	[illegible]	[illegible]	[illegible]	[illegible]	[illegible]
Donegal,	[illegible]	[illegible]	[illegible]	[illegible]	[illegible]	[illegible]
Down,	[illegible]	[illegible]	[illegible]	[illegible]	[illegible]	[illegible]
Fermanagh,	[illegible]	[illegible]	[illegible]	[illegible]	[illegible]	[illegible]
Londonderry,	[illegible]	[illegible]	[illegible]	[illegible]	[illegible]	[illegible]
Monaghan,	[illegible]	[illegible]	[illegible]	[illegible]	[illegible]	[illegible]
Tyrone,	[illegible]	[illegible]	[illegible]	[illegible]	[illegible]	[illegible]
Total,	[illegible]	[illegible]	[illegible]	[illegible]	[illegible]	[illegible]
Leinster:						
Carlow,	[illegible]	[illegible]	[illegible]	[illegible]	[illegible]	[illegible]
Dublin,	[illegible]	[illegible]	[illegible]	[illegible]	[illegible]	[illegible]
Kildare,	[illegible]	[illegible]	[illegible]	[illegible]	[illegible]	[illegible]
Kilkenny,	[illegible]	[illegible]	[illegible]	[illegible]	[illegible]	[illegible]
King's,	[illegible]	[illegible]	[illegible]	[illegible]	[illegible]	[illegible]
Longford,	[illegible]	[illegible]	[illegible]	[illegible]	[illegible]	[illegible]
Louth,	[illegible]	[illegible]	[illegible]	[illegible]	[illegible]	[illegible]
Meath,	[illegible]	[illegible]	[illegible]	[illegible]	[illegible]	[illegible]
Queen's,	[illegible]	[illegible]	[illegible]	[illegible]	[illegible]	[illegible]
Westmeath,	[illegible]	[illegible]	[illegible]	[illegible]	[illegible]	[illegible]
Wexford,	[illegible]	[illegible]	[illegible]	[illegible]	[illegible]	[illegible]
Wicklow,	[illegible]	[illegible]	[illegible]	[illegible]	[illegible]	[illegible]
Total,	[illegible]	[illegible]	[illegible]	[illegible]	[illegible]	[illegible]
Connaught:						
Galway,	[illegible]	[illegible]	[illegible]	[illegible]	[illegible]	[illegible]
Leitrim,	[illegible]	[illegible]	[illegible]	[illegible]	[illegible]	[illegible]
Mayo,	[illegible]	[illegible]	[illegible]	[illegible]	[illegible]	[illegible]
Roscommon,	[illegible]	[illegible]	[illegible]	[illegible]	[illegible]	[illegible]
Sligo,	[illegible]	[illegible]	[illegible]	[illegible]	[illegible]	[illegible]
Total,	[illegible]	[illegible]	[illegible]	[illegible]	[illegible]	[illegible]
Munster:						
Clare,	[illegible]	[illegible]	[illegible]	[illegible]	[illegible]	[illegible]
Cork,	[illegible]	[illegible]	[illegible]	[illegible]	[illegible]	[illegible]
Kerry,	[illegible]	[illegible]	[illegible]	[illegible]	[illegible]	[illegible]
Limerick,	[illegible]	[illegible]	[illegible]	[illegible]	[illegible]	[illegible]
Tipperary,	[illegible]	[illegible]	[illegible]	[illegible]	[illegible]	[illegible]
Waterford,	[illegible]	[illegible]	[illegible]	[illegible]	[illegible]	[illegible]
Total,	[illegible]	[illegible]	[illegible]	[illegible]	[illegible]	[illegible]
SUMMARY.						
Ulster,	[illegible]	[illegible]	[illegible]	[illegible]	[illegible]	[illegible]
Leinster,	[illegible]	[illegible]	[illegible]	[illegible]	[illegible]	[illegible]
Connaught,	[illegible]	[illegible]	[illegible]	[illegible]	[illegible]	[illegible]
Munster,	[illegible]	[illegible]	[illegible]	[illegible]	[illegible]	[illegible]
Total,	[illegible]	[illegible]	[illegible]	[illegible]	[illegible]	[illegible]

—Table showing, according to Provinces and Counties, the Number of Cases in which Judicial Rents have been fixed for Individual Tenancies by Chief Commissioners and Sub-Commissioners during the year ended the 21st August, 1890; and also a Summary of the Acreage, Tenement Valuations, Former Rents and Judicial Rents of the Holdings, and the Per-centages of Reductions made in the former Rents.

Province and County.	Number of Cases in which Judicial Rents have been fixed.	Acreage. Statute Acres.	Tenement Valuation.	Former Rent.	Judicial Rent.	Per-centage of Reduction.
		A. R. P.	£ s. d.	£ s. d.	£ s. d.	
ULSTER:						
Antrim,	[illegible]	[illegible]	[illegible]	[illegible]	[illegible]	[illegible]
Armagh,	[illegible]	[illegible]	[illegible]	[illegible]	[illegible]	[illegible]
Cavan,	[illegible]	[illegible]	[illegible]	[illegible]	[illegible]	[illegible]
Donegal,	[illegible]	[illegible]	[illegible]	[illegible]	[illegible]	[illegible]
Down,	[illegible]	[illegible]	[illegible]	[illegible]	[illegible]	[illegible]
Fermanagh,	[illegible]	[illegible]	[illegible]	[illegible]	[illegible]	[illegible]
Londonderry,	[illegible]	[illegible]	[illegible]	[illegible]	[illegible]	[illegible]
Monaghan,	[illegible]	[illegible]	[illegible]	[illegible]	[illegible]	[illegible]
Tyrone,	[illegible]	[illegible]	[illegible]	[illegible]	[illegible]	[illegible]
Total,	[illegible]	[illegible]	[illegible]	[illegible]	[illegible]	[illegible]
LEINSTER:						
Carlow,	[illegible]	[illegible]	[illegible]	[illegible]	[illegible]	[illegible]
Dublin,	[illegible]	[illegible]	[illegible]	[illegible]	[illegible]	[illegible]
Kildare,	[illegible]	[illegible]	[illegible]	[illegible]	[illegible]	[illegible]
Kilkenny,	[illegible]	[illegible]	[illegible]	[illegible]	[illegible]	[illegible]
King's,	[illegible]	[illegible]	[illegible]	[illegible]	[illegible]	[illegible]
Longford,	[illegible]	[illegible]	[illegible]	[illegible]	[illegible]	[illegible]
Louth,	[illegible]	[illegible]	[illegible]	[illegible]	[illegible]	[illegible]
Meath,	[illegible]	[illegible]	[illegible]	[illegible]	[illegible]	[illegible]
Queen's,	[illegible]	[illegible]	[illegible]	[illegible]	[illegible]	[illegible]
Westmeath,	[illegible]	[illegible]	[illegible]	[illegible]	[illegible]	[illegible]
Wexford,	[illegible]	[illegible]	[illegible]	[illegible]	[illegible]	[illegible]
Wicklow,	[illegible]	[illegible]	[illegible]	[illegible]	[illegible]	[illegible]
Total,	[illegible]	[illegible]	[illegible]	[illegible]	[illegible]	[illegible]
CONNAUGHT:						
Galway,	[illegible]	[illegible]	[illegible]	[illegible]	[illegible]	[illegible]
Leitrim,	[illegible]	[illegible]	[illegible]	[illegible]	[illegible]	[illegible]
Mayo,	[illegible]	[illegible]	[illegible]	[illegible]	[illegible]	[illegible]
Roscommon,	[illegible]	[illegible]	[illegible]	[illegible]	[illegible]	[illegible]
Sligo,	[illegible]	[illegible]	[illegible]	[illegible]	[illegible]	[illegible]
Total,	[illegible]	[illegible]	[illegible]	[illegible]	[illegible]	[illegible]
MUNSTER:						
Clare,	[illegible]	[illegible]	[illegible]	[illegible]	[illegible]	[illegible]
Cork,	[illegible]	[illegible]	[illegible]	[illegible]	[illegible]	[illegible]

VI.—TABLE showing, according to Provinces and Counties, the Number of Cases in which Judicial Rents have been fixed for Leasehold Tenancies, by Chief Commission and Sub-Commissions during the Three Years ended the 31st August, 1890; and also a Summary of the Acreage, Tenement Valuations, Former Rents, Judicial Rents of the Holdings, and the Percentages of Reductions made in the former Rents.

Province and County.	Number of Cases in which Judicial Rents have been fixed.	Acreage, Statute Acres.	Tenement Valuation.	Former Rent.	Judicial Rent.	Percentage of Reduction.
		A. R. P.	£ s. d.	£ s. d.	£ s. d.	
ULSTER:						
Antrim,	[illegible]	[illegible]	[illegible]	[illegible]	[illegible]	[illegible]
Armagh,	[illegible]	[illegible]	[illegible]	[illegible]	[illegible]	[illegible]
Cavan,	[illegible]	[illegible]	[illegible]	[illegible]	[illegible]	[illegible]
Donegal,	[illegible]	[illegible]	[illegible]	[illegible]	[illegible]	[illegible]
Down,	[illegible]	[illegible]	[illegible]	[illegible]	[illegible]	[illegible]
Fermanagh,	[illegible]	[illegible]	[illegible]	[illegible]	[illegible]	[illegible]
Londonderry,	[illegible]	[illegible]	[illegible]	[illegible]	[illegible]	[illegible]
Monaghan,	[illegible]	[illegible]	[illegible]	[illegible]	[illegible]	[illegible]
Tyrone,	[illegible]	[illegible]	[illegible]	[illegible]	[illegible]	[illegible]
Total,	[illegible]	[illegible]	[illegible]	[illegible]	[illegible]	[illegible]
LEINSTER:						
Carlow,	[illegible]	[illegible]	[illegible]	[illegible]	[illegible]	[illegible]
Dublin,	[illegible]	[illegible]	[illegible]	[illegible]	[illegible]	[illegible]
Kildare,	[illegible]	[illegible]	[illegible]	[illegible]	[illegible]	[illegible]
Kilkenny,	[illegible]	[illegible]	[illegible]	[illegible]	[illegible]	[illegible]
King's,	[illegible]	[illegible]	[illegible]	[illegible]	[illegible]	[illegible]
Longford,	[illegible]	[illegible]	[illegible]	[illegible]	[illegible]	[illegible]
Louth,	[illegible]	[illegible]	[illegible]	[illegible]	[illegible]	[illegible]
Meath,	[illegible]	[illegible]	[illegible]	[illegible]	[illegible]	[illegible]
Queen's,	[illegible]	[illegible]	[illegible]	[illegible]	[illegible]	[illegible]
Westmeath,	[illegible]	[illegible]	[illegible]	[illegible]	[illegible]	[illegible]
Wexford,	[illegible]	[illegible]	[illegible]	[illegible]	[illegible]	[illegible]
Wicklow,	[illegible]	[illegible]	[illegible]	[illegible]	[illegible]	[illegible]
Total,	[illegible]	[illegible]	[illegible]	[illegible]	[illegible]	[illegible]
CONNAUGHT:						
Galway,	[illegible]	[illegible]	[illegible]	[illegible]	[illegible]	[illegible]
Leitrim,	[illegible]	[illegible]	[illegible]	[illegible]	[illegible]	[illegible]
Mayo,	[illegible]	[illegible]	[illegible]	[illegible]	[illegible]	[illegible]
Roscommon,	[illegible]	[illegible]	[illegible]	[illegible]	[illegible]	[illegible]
Sligo,	[illegible]	[illegible]	[illegible]	[illegible]	[illegible]	[illegible]
Total,	[illegible]	[illegible]	[illegible]	[illegible]	[illegible]	[illegible]
MUNSTER:						
Clare,	[illegible]	[illegible]	[illegible]	[illegible]	[illegible]	[illegible]
Cork,	[illegible]	[illegible]	[illegible]	[illegible]	[illegible]	[illegible]
Kerry,	[illegible]	[illegible]	[illegible]	[illegible]	[illegible]	[illegible]
Limerick,	[illegible]	[illegible]	[illegible]	[illegible]	[illegible]	[illegible]
Tipperary,	[illegible]	[illegible]	[illegible]	[illegible]	[illegible]	[illegible]
Waterford,	[illegible]	[illegible]	[illegible]	[illegible]	[illegible]	[illegible]
Total,	[illegible]	[illegible]	[illegible]	[illegible]	[illegible]	[illegible]
SUMMARY:						
ULSTER,	[illegible]	[illegible]	[illegible]	[illegible]	[illegible]	[illegible]
LEINSTER,	[illegible]	[illegible]	[illegible]	[illegible]	[illegible]	[illegible]
CONNAUGHT,	[illegible]	[illegible]	[illegible]	[illegible]	[illegible]	[illegible]
MUNSTER,	[illegible]	[illegible]	[illegible]	[illegible]	[illegible]	[illegible]
Total,	[illegible]	[illegible]	[illegible]	[illegible]	[illegible]	[illegible]

VII.—TABLE showing, according to Provinces and Counties, the Number of Cases in which Judicial Rents have been fixed by the Irish Land Commission on the Reports of Valuers appointed upon the applications of Landlords and Tenants, during the year ended the 31st August, 1890; and also a Summary of the Acreage, Tenement Valuations, Former Rents, Judicial Rents of the Holdings, and the Per-centages of Reductions made in the Former Rents.

Province and County.	Number of Cases in which Judicial Rents have been fixed.	Acreage. Statute Acres.	Tenement Valuation.	Former Rent.	Judicial Rent.	Per Centage of Reductions.
		a. r. p.	£ s. d.	£ s. d.	£ s. d.	
Ulster:						
Antrim,	[illegible]	[illegible]	[illegible]	[illegible]	[illegible]	[illegible]
Armagh,	—	—	—	—	—	—
Cavan,	—	—	—	—	—	—
Donegal,	—	—	—	—	—	—
Down,	—	—	—	—	—	—
Fermanagh,	—	—	—	—	—	—
Londonderry,	—	—	—	—	—	—
Monaghan,	—	—	—	—	—	—
Tyrone,	—	—	—	—	—	—
Total,	[illegible]	[illegible]	[illegible]	[illegible]	[illegible]	[illegible]
Leinster:						
Carlow,	[illegible]	[illegible]	[illegible]	[illegible]	[illegible]	[illegible]
Dublin,	—	—	—	—	—	—
Kildare,	[illegible]	[illegible]	[illegible]	[illegible]	[illegible]	[illegible]
Kilkenny,	—	—	—	—	—	—
King's,	[illegible]	[illegible]	[illegible]	[illegible]	[illegible]	[illegible]
Longford,	—	—	—	—	—	—
Louth,	—	—	—	—	—	—
Meath,	[illegible]	[illegible]	[illegible]	[illegible]	[illegible]	[illegible]
Queen's,	—	—	—	—	—	—
Westmeath,	—	—	—	—	—	—
Wexford,	—	—	—	—	—	—
Wicklow,	[illegible]	[illegible]	[illegible]	[illegible]	[illegible]	[illegible]
Total,	[illegible]	[illegible]	[illegible]	[illegible]	[illegible]	[illegible]
Connaught:						
Galway,	—	—	—	—	—	—
Leitrim,	—	—	—	—	—	—
Mayo,	—	—	—	—	—	—
Roscommon,	—	—	—	—	—	—
Sligo,	—	—	—	—	—	—
Total,	—	—	—	—	—	—
Munster:						
Clare,	[illegible]	[illegible]	[illegible]	[illegible]	[illegible]	[illegible]
Cork,	[illegible]	[illegible]	[illegible]	[illegible]	[illegible]	[illegible]
Kerry,	—	—	—	—	—	—
Limerick,	[illegible]	[illegible]	[illegible]	[illegible]	[illegible]	[illegible]
Tipperary,	[illegible]	[illegible]	[illegible]	[illegible]	[illegible]	[illegible]
Waterford,	[illegible]	[illegible]	[illegible]	[illegible]	[illegible]	[illegible]
Total,	[illegible]	[illegible]	[illegible]	[illegible]	[illegible]	[illegible]
SUMMARY.						
Ulster,	[illegible]	[illegible]	[illegible]	[illegible]	[illegible]	[illegible]
Leinster,	[illegible]	[illegible]	[illegible]	[illegible]	[illegible]	[illegible]
Connaught,	—	—	—	—	—	—
Munster,	[illegible]	[illegible]	[illegible]	[illegible]	[illegible]	[illegible]
Total,	[illegible]	[illegible]	[illegible]	[illegible]	[illegible]	[illegible]

VIII.—TABLE showing, according to Provinces and Counties, the Number of Cases in which Judicial Rents have been fixed by the Irish Land Commission on the Reports of Valuers appointed upon the applications of Landlords and Tenants, from the 25th May, 1888, to the 31st August, 1890; and also, a Summary of the Acreage, Tenement Valuations, Former Rents, Judicial Rents of the Holdings, and the Per-centages of Reductions made in the Former Rents.

Province and County.	Number of Cases in which Judicial Rents have been fixed.	Acreage. Statute Measure.	Tenement Valuation.	Former Rent.	Judicial Rent.	Percentage of Reduction.
		A. R. P.	£ s. d.	£ s. d.	£ s. d.	
ULSTER:—						
Antrim,	[illegible]	[illegible]	[illegible]	[illegible]	[illegible]	[illegible]
Armagh,	—	—	—	—	—	—
Cavan,	[illegible]	[illegible]	[illegible]	[illegible]	[illegible]	[illegible]
Donegal,	[illegible]	[illegible]	[illegible]	[illegible]	[illegible]	[illegible]
Down,	—	—	—	—	—	—
Fermanagh,	[illegible]	[illegible]	[illegible]	[illegible]	[illegible]	[illegible]
Londonderry,	—	—	—	—	—	—
Monaghan,	[illegible]	[illegible]	[illegible]	[illegible]	[illegible]	[illegible]
Tyrone,	[illegible]	[illegible]	[illegible]	[illegible]	[illegible]	[illegible]
Total,	[illegible]	[illegible]	[illegible]	[illegible]	[illegible]	[illegible]
LEINSTER:—						
Carlow,	[illegible]	[illegible]	[illegible]	[illegible]	[illegible]	[illegible]
Dublin,	[illegible]	[illegible]	—	[illegible]	[illegible]	[illegible]
Kildare,	[illegible]	[illegible]	[illegible]	[illegible]	[illegible]	[illegible]
Kilkenny,	[illegible]	[illegible]	[illegible]	[illegible]	[illegible]	[illegible]
King's,	[illegible]	[illegible]	[illegible]	[illegible]	[illegible]	[illegible]
Longford,	[illegible]	[illegible]	[illegible]	[illegible]	[illegible]	[illegible]
Louth,*	[illegible]	[illegible]	[illegible]	[illegible]	[illegible]	[illegible]
Meath,	[illegible]	[illegible]	[illegible]	[illegible]	[illegible]	[illegible]
Queen's,	[illegible]	[illegible]	[illegible]	[illegible]	[illegible]	[illegible]
Westmeath,	[illegible]	[illegible]	[illegible]	[illegible]	[illegible]	[illegible]
Wexford,	[illegible]	[illegible]	[illegible]	[illegible]	[illegible]	[illegible]
Wicklow,	[illegible]	[illegible]	[illegible]	[illegible]	[illegible]	[illegible]
Total,	[illegible]	[illegible]	[illegible]	[illegible]	[illegible]	[illegible]
CONNAUGHT:—						
Galway,	[illegible]	[illegible]	[illegible]	[illegible]	[illegible]	[illegible]
Leitrim,	[illegible]	[illegible]	[illegible]	[illegible]	[illegible]	[illegible]
Mayo,	[illegible]	[illegible]	[illegible]	[illegible]	[illegible]	[illegible]
Roscommon,	[illegible]	[illegible]	[illegible]	[illegible]	[illegible]	[illegible]
Sligo,	[illegible]	[illegible]	[illegible]	[illegible]	[illegible]	[illegible]
Total,	[illegible]	[illegible]	[illegible]	[illegible]	[illegible]	[illegible]
MUNSTER:—						
Clare,	[illegible]	[illegible]	[illegible]	[illegible]	[illegible]	[illegible]
Cork,	[illegible]	[illegible]	[illegible]	[illegible]	[illegible]	[illegible]
Kerry,	[illegible]	[illegible]	[illegible]	[illegible]	[illegible]	[illegible]
Limerick,	[illegible]	[illegible]	[illegible]	[illegible]	[illegible]	[illegible]
Tipperary,	[illegible]	[illegible]	[illegible]	[illegible]	[illegible]	[illegible]
Waterford,	[illegible]	[illegible]	[illegible]	[illegible]	[illegible]	[illegible]
Total,	[illegible]	[illegible]	[illegible]	[illegible]	[illegible]	[illegible]
SUMMARY.						
Ulster,	[illegible]	[illegible]	[illegible]	[illegible]	[illegible]	[illegible]
Leinster,	[illegible]	[illegible]	[illegible]	[illegible]	[illegible]	[illegible]
Connaught,	[illegible]	[illegible]	[illegible]	[illegible]	[illegible]	[illegible]
Munster,	[illegible]	[illegible]	[illegible]	[illegible]	[illegible]	[illegible]
Total,	[illegible]	[illegible]	[illegible]	[illegible]	[illegible]	[illegible]

* [illegible]

IX.—Table showing, according to Provinces and Counties, the Number of Originating Notices to fix Fair Rents lodged with the Civil Bill Courts, the Number of such Notices transferred to the Irish Land Commission, the number of Rents Fixed, and of Cases Dismissed, Struck Out, and Withdrawn, as notified to the Irish Land Commission, during the year ended 31st August, 1880.

Province and County.	Number of Originating Notices to fix Fair Rents lodged.		Number transferred to Irish Land Commission.		Number of Rents Fixed.		Number of Applications Dismissed, Struck Out, and Withdrawn.	Total Number of Cases disposed of.
	Yearly Tenancies.	Leasehold Tenancies.	Yearly Tenancies.	Leasehold Tenancies.	Yearly Tenancies.	Leasehold Tenancies.		
Ulster:								
Antrim,	[illegible]	[illegible]	[illegible]	[illegible]	[illegible]	[illegible]	[illegible]	[illegible]
Armagh,	[illegible]	[illegible]	[illegible]	[illegible]	[illegible]	[illegible]	[illegible]	[illegible]
Cavan,	[illegible]	[illegible]	[illegible]	[illegible]	[illegible]	[illegible]	[illegible]	[illegible]
Donegal,	[illegible]	[illegible]	[illegible]	[illegible]	[illegible]	[illegible]	[illegible]	[illegible]
Down,	[illegible]	[illegible]	[illegible]	[illegible]	[illegible]	[illegible]	[illegible]	[illegible]
Fermanagh,	[illegible]	[illegible]	[illegible]	[illegible]	[illegible]	[illegible]	[illegible]	[illegible]
Londonderry,	[illegible]	[illegible]	[illegible]	[illegible]	[illegible]	[illegible]	[illegible]	[illegible]
Monaghan,	[illegible]	[illegible]	[illegible]	[illegible]	[illegible]	[illegible]	[illegible]	[illegible]
Tyrone,	[illegible]	[illegible]	[illegible]	[illegible]	[illegible]	[illegible]	[illegible]	[illegible]
Total,	[illegible]	[illegible]	[illegible]	[illegible]	[illegible]	[illegible]	[illegible]	[illegible]
Leinster:								
Carlow,	[illegible]	[illegible]	[illegible]	[illegible]	[illegible]	[illegible]	[illegible]	[illegible]
Dublin,	[illegible]	[illegible]	[illegible]	[illegible]	[illegible]	[illegible]	[illegible]	[illegible]
Kildare,	[illegible]	[illegible]	[illegible]	[illegible]	[illegible]	[illegible]	[illegible]	[illegible]
Kilkenny,	[illegible]	[illegible]	[illegible]	[illegible]	[illegible]	[illegible]	[illegible]	[illegible]
King's,	[illegible]	[illegible]	[illegible]	[illegible]	[illegible]	[illegible]	[illegible]	[illegible]
Longford,	[illegible]	[illegible]	[illegible]	[illegible]	[illegible]	[illegible]	[illegible]	[illegible]
Louth,	[illegible]	[illegible]	[illegible]	[illegible]	[illegible]	[illegible]	[illegible]	[illegible]
Meath,	[illegible]	[illegible]	[illegible]	[illegible]	[illegible]	[illegible]	[illegible]	[illegible]
Queen's,	[illegible]	[illegible]	[illegible]	[illegible]	[illegible]	[illegible]	[illegible]	[illegible]
Westmeath,	[illegible]	[illegible]	[illegible]	[illegible]	[illegible]	[illegible]	[illegible]	[illegible]
Wexford,	[illegible]	[illegible]	[illegible]	[illegible]	[illegible]	[illegible]	[illegible]	[illegible]
Wicklow,	[illegible]	[illegible]	[illegible]	[illegible]	[illegible]	[illegible]	[illegible]	[illegible]
Total,	[illegible]	[illegible]	[illegible]	[illegible]	[illegible]	[illegible]	[illegible]	[illegible]
Connaught:								
Galway,	[illegible]	[illegible]	[illegible]	[illegible]	[illegible]	[illegible]	[illegible]	[illegible]
Leitrim,	[illegible]	[illegible]	[illegible]	[illegible]	[illegible]	[illegible]	[illegible]	[illegible]
Mayo,	[illegible]	[illegible]	[illegible]	[illegible]	[illegible]	[illegible]	[illegible]	[illegible]
Roscommon,	[illegible]	[illegible]	[illegible]	[illegible]	[illegible]	[illegible]	[illegible]	[illegible]
Sligo,	[illegible]	[illegible]	[illegible]	[illegible]	[illegible]	[illegible]	[illegible]	[illegible]
Total,	[illegible]	[illegible]	[illegible]	[illegible]	[illegible]	[illegible]	[illegible]	[illegible]

X.—TABLE showing, according to Provinces and Counties, the Number of Originating Notices to fix Fair Rents lodged with the Civil Bill Courts, the Number of such Notices transferred to the Irish Land Commission, the Number of Rents Fixed, and of Cases Dismissed, Struck Out, and Withdrawn, as notified to the Irish Land Commission, during the nine years ended 21st August, 1890.

PROVINCE AND COUNTY.	Number of Originating Notices to fix Fair Rents lodged.		Total Number of Cases.	Number transferred to Irish Land Commission.		Number of Rents Fixed.		Number of Applications Dismissed, Struck Out, and Withdrawn.	Total Number of Cases disposed of.	[illegible]
	Yearly Tenancies.	Leasehold Tenancies.		Yearly Tenancies.	Leasehold Tenancies.	Yearly Tenancies.	Leasehold Tenancies.			
ULSTER:										
Antrim,	17	[illegible]	[illegible]	[illegible]	[illegible]	[illegible]	[illegible]	[illegible]	[illegible]	[illegible]
Armagh,	[illegible]	[illegible]	[illegible]	[illegible]	[illegible]	[illegible]	[illegible]	[illegible]	[illegible]	[illegible]
Cavan,	[illegible]	[illegible]	[illegible]	[illegible]	[illegible]	[illegible]	[illegible]	[illegible]	[illegible]	[illegible]
Donegal,	[illegible]	[illegible]	[illegible]	[illegible]	[illegible]	[illegible]	[illegible]	[illegible]	[illegible]	[illegible]
Down,	[illegible]	[illegible]	[illegible]	[illegible]	[illegible]	[illegible]	[illegible]	[illegible]	[illegible]	[illegible]
Fermanagh,	[illegible]	[illegible]	[illegible]	[illegible]	[illegible]	[illegible]	[illegible]	[illegible]	[illegible]	[illegible]
Londonderry,	[illegible]	[illegible]	[illegible]	[illegible]	[illegible]	[illegible]	[illegible]	[illegible]	[illegible]	[illegible]
Monaghan,	[illegible]	[illegible]	[illegible]	[illegible]	[illegible]	[illegible]	[illegible]	[illegible]	[illegible]	[illegible]
Tyrone,	[illegible]	[illegible]	[illegible]	[illegible]	[illegible]	[illegible]	[illegible]	[illegible]	[illegible]	[illegible]
Total,	[illegible]	[illegible]	[illegible]	[illegible]	[illegible]	[illegible]	[illegible]	[illegible]	[illegible]	[illegible]
LEINSTER:										
Carlow,	[illegible]	[illegible]	[illegible]	[illegible]	[illegible]	[illegible]	[illegible]	[illegible]	[illegible]	[illegible]
Dublin,	[illegible]	[illegible]	[illegible]	[illegible]	[illegible]	[illegible]	[illegible]	[illegible]	[illegible]	[illegible]
Kildare,	[illegible]	[illegible]	[illegible]	[illegible]	[illegible]	[illegible]	[illegible]	[illegible]	[illegible]	[illegible]
Kilkenny,	[illegible]	[illegible]	[illegible]	[illegible]	[illegible]	[illegible]	[illegible]	[illegible]	[illegible]	[illegible]
King's,	[illegible]	[illegible]	[illegible]	[illegible]	[illegible]	[illegible]	[illegible]	[illegible]	[illegible]	[illegible]
Longford,	[illegible]	[illegible]	[illegible]	[illegible]	[illegible]	[illegible]	[illegible]	[illegible]	[illegible]	[illegible]
Louth,	[illegible]	[illegible]	[illegible]	[illegible]	[illegible]	[illegible]	[illegible]	[illegible]	[illegible]	[illegible]
Meath,	[illegible]	[illegible]	[illegible]	[illegible]	[illegible]	[illegible]	[illegible]	[illegible]	[illegible]	[illegible]
Queen's,	[illegible]	[illegible]	[illegible]	[illegible]	[illegible]	[illegible]	[illegible]	[illegible]	[illegible]	[illegible]
Westmeath,	[illegible]	[illegible]	[illegible]	[illegible]	[illegible]	[illegible]	[illegible]	[illegible]	[illegible]	[illegible]
Wexford,	[illegible]	[illegible]	[illegible]	[illegible]	[illegible]	[illegible]	[illegible]	[illegible]	[illegible]	[illegible]
Wicklow,	[illegible]	[illegible]	[illegible]	[illegible]	[illegible]	[illegible]	[illegible]	[illegible]	[illegible]	[illegible]
Total,	[illegible]	[illegible]	[illegible]	[illegible]	[illegible]	[illegible]	[illegible]	[illegible]	[illegible]	[illegible]
CONNAUGHT:										
Galway,	[illegible]	[illegible]	[illegible]	[illegible]	[illegible]	[illegible]	[illegible]	[illegible]	[illegible]	[illegible]
Leitrim,	[illegible]	[illegible]	[illegible]	[illegible]	[illegible]	[illegible]	[illegible]	[illegible]	[illegible]	[illegible]
Mayo,	[illegible]	[illegible]	[illegible]	[illegible]	[illegible]	[illegible]	[illegible]	[illegible]	[illegible]	[illegible]
Roscommon,	[illegible]	[illegible]	[illegible]	[illegible]	[illegible]	[illegible]	[illegible]	[illegible]	[illegible]	[illegible]
Sligo,	[illegible]	[illegible]	[illegible]	[illegible]	[illegible]	[illegible]	[illegible]	[illegible]	[illegible]	[illegible]
Total,	[illegible]	[illegible]	[illegible]	[illegible]	[illegible]	[illegible]	[illegible]	[illegible]	[illegible]	[illegible]
MUNSTER:										
Clare,	[illegible]	[illegible]	[illegible]	[illegible]	[illegible]	[illegible]	[illegible]	[illegible]	[illegible]	[illegible]
Cork,	[illegible]	[illegible]	[illegible]	[illegible]	[illegible]	[illegible]	[illegible]	[illegible]	[illegible]	[illegible]
Kerry,	[illegible]	[illegible]	[illegible]	[illegible]	[illegible]	[illegible]	[illegible]	[illegible]	[illegible]	[illegible]
Limerick,	[illegible]	[illegible]	[illegible]	[illegible]	[illegible]	[illegible]	[illegible]	[illegible]	[illegible]	[illegible]
Tipperary,	[illegible]	[illegible]	[illegible]	[illegible]	[illegible]	[illegible]	[illegible]	[illegible]	[illegible]	[illegible]
Waterford,	[illegible]	[illegible]	[illegible]	[illegible]	[illegible]	[illegible]	[illegible]	[illegible]	[illegible]	[illegible]
Total,	[illegible]	[illegible]	[illegible]	[illegible]	[illegible]	[illegible]	[illegible]	[illegible]	[illegible]	[illegible]
SUMMARY.										
Ulster,	[illegible]	[illegible]	[illegible]	[illegible]	[illegible]	[illegible]	[illegible]	[illegible]	[illegible]	[illegible]
Leinster,	[illegible]	[illegible]	[illegible]	[illegible]	[illegible]	[illegible]	[illegible]	[illegible]	[illegible]	[illegible]
Connaught,	[illegible]	[illegible]	[illegible]	[illegible]	[illegible]	[illegible]	[illegible]	[illegible]	[illegible]	[illegible]
Munster,	[illegible]	[illegible]	[illegible]	[illegible]	[illegible]	[illegible]	[illegible]	[illegible]	[illegible]	[illegible]
Total,	[illegible]	[illegible]	[illegible]	[illegible]	[illegible]	[illegible]	[illegible]	[illegible]	[illegible]	[illegible]

XI.—Table showing, according to Provinces and Counties, the Number of Cases in which Judicial Rents have been fixed, for Yearly Tenancies, by Civil Bill Courts, as notified to the Irish Land Commission, during the year ended 21st August, [illegible], and also a Summary of the Average Tenement Valuations, Former Rents, and Judicial Rents of the Holdings, and the Percentages of Reductions made in the Former Rents.

Provinces and Counties.	No. of Cases in which Judicial Rents have been fixed.	Average Statute Acres.	Tenement Valuation.	Former Rent.	Judicial Rent.	Percentages of Reduction.
Ulster:		a. r. p.	£ s. d.	£ s. d.	£ s. d.	
Antrim,	—	—	—	—	—	—
Armagh,	[illegible]	[illegible]	[illegible]	[illegible]	[illegible]	[illegible]
Cavan,	[illegible]	[illegible]	[illegible]	[illegible]	[illegible]	[illegible]
Donegal,	[illegible]	[illegible]	[illegible]	[illegible]	[illegible]	[illegible]
Down,	[illegible]	[illegible]	[illegible]	[illegible]	[illegible]	[illegible]
Fermanagh,	[illegible]	[illegible]	[illegible]	[illegible]	[illegible]	[illegible]
Londonderry,	[illegible]	[illegible]	[illegible]	[illegible]	[illegible]	[illegible]
Monaghan,	—	—	—	—	—	—
Tyrone,	[illegible]	[illegible]	[illegible]	[illegible]	[illegible]	[illegible]
Total,	[illegible]	[illegible]	[illegible]	[illegible]	[illegible]	[illegible]
Leinster:						
Carlow,	—	—	—	—	—	—
Dublin,	—	—	—	—	—	—
Kildare,	[illegible]	[illegible]	[illegible]	[illegible]	[illegible]	[illegible]
Kilkenny,	[illegible]	[illegible]	[illegible]	[illegible]	[illegible]	[illegible]
King's,	[illegible]	[illegible]	[illegible]	[illegible]	[illegible]	[illegible]
Longford,	[illegible]	[illegible]	[illegible]	[illegible]	[illegible]	[illegible]
Louth,	[illegible]	[illegible]	[illegible]	[illegible]	[illegible]	[illegible]
Meath,	[illegible]	[illegible]	[illegible]	[illegible]	[illegible]	[illegible]
Queen's,	—	—	—	—	—	—
Westmeath,	[illegible]	[illegible]	[illegible]	[illegible]	[illegible]	[illegible]
Wexford,	—	—	—	—	—	—
Wicklow,	—	—	—	—	—	—
Total,	[illegible]	[illegible]	[illegible]	[illegible]	[illegible]	[illegible]
Connaught:						
Galway,	[illegible]	[illegible]	[illegible]	[illegible]	[illegible]	[illegible]
Leitrim,	[illegible]	[illegible]	[illegible]	[illegible]	[illegible]	[illegible]
Mayo,	[illegible]	[illegible]	[illegible]	[illegible]	[illegible]	[illegible]
Roscommon,	[illegible]	[illegible]	[illegible]	[illegible]	[illegible]	[illegible]
Sligo,	—	—	—	—	—	—
Total,	[illegible]	[illegible]	[illegible]	[illegible]	[illegible]	[illegible]
Munster:						
Clare,	—	—	—	—	—	—
Cork,	[illegible]	[illegible]	[illegible]	[illegible]	[illegible]	[illegible]
Kerry,	[illegible]	[illegible]	[illegible]	[illegible]	[illegible]	[illegible]
Limerick,	[illegible]	[illegible]	[illegible]	[illegible]	[illegible]	[illegible]
Tipperary,	[illegible]	[illegible]	[illegible]	[illegible]	[illegible]	[illegible]
Waterford,	[illegible]	[illegible]	[illegible]	[illegible]	[illegible]	[illegible]
Total,	[illegible]	[illegible]	[illegible]	[illegible]	[illegible]	[illegible]
SUMMARY.						
Ulster,	[illegible]	[illegible]	[illegible]	[illegible]	[illegible]	[illegible]
Leinster,	[illegible]	[illegible]	[illegible]	[illegible]	[illegible]	[illegible]
Connaught,	[illegible]	[illegible]	[illegible]	[illegible]	[illegible]	[illegible]
Munster,	[illegible]	[illegible]	[illegible]	[illegible]	[illegible]	[illegible]
Total,	[illegible]	[illegible]	[illegible]	[illegible]	[illegible]	[illegible]

XII.—Table showing, according to Provinces and Counties, the Number of Cases in which Judicial Rents for Yearly Tenancies have been fixed by Civil Bill Courts, as notified to the Irish Land Commission during the [illegible] Years ended 31st August, [illegible]; and also a Summary of the Acreage, Tenement Valuations, Former Rents, Judicial Rents of the Holdings, and the Per-centages of Reductions made in the Former Rents.

Provinces and Counties.	Number of Cases in which Judicial Rents have been fixed.	Average Statute Acres.	Tenement Valuation.	Former Rent.	Judicial Rent.	Per-centage of Reduction.
		A. R. P.	£ s. d.	£ s. d.	£ s. d.	
Ulster:						
Antrim,	—	—	—	—	—	—
Armagh,	[illegible]	[illegible]	[illegible]	[illegible]	[illegible]	[illegible]
Cavan,	[illegible]	[illegible]	[illegible]	[illegible]	[illegible]	[illegible]
Donegal,	[illegible]	[illegible]	[illegible]	[illegible]	[illegible]	[illegible]
Down,	[illegible]	[illegible]	[illegible]	[illegible]	[illegible]	[illegible]
Fermanagh,	[illegible]	[illegible]	[illegible]	[illegible]	[illegible]	[illegible]
Londonderry,	[illegible]	[illegible]	[illegible]	[illegible]	[illegible]	[illegible]
Monaghan,	[illegible]	[illegible]	[illegible]	[illegible]	[illegible]	[illegible]
Tyrone,	[illegible]	[illegible]	[illegible]	[illegible]	[illegible]	[illegible]
Total,	[illegible]	[illegible]	[illegible]	[illegible]	[illegible]	[illegible]
Leinster:						
Carlow,	[illegible]	[illegible]	[illegible]	[illegible]	[illegible]	[illegible]
Dublin,	—	—	—	—	—	—
Kildare,	[illegible]	[illegible]	[illegible]	[illegible]	[illegible]	[illegible]
Kilkenny,	[illegible]	[illegible]	[illegible]	[illegible]	[illegible]	[illegible]
King's,	[illegible]	[illegible]	[illegible]	[illegible]	[illegible]	[illegible]
Longford,	[illegible]	[illegible]	[illegible]	[illegible]	[illegible]	[illegible]
Louth,	[illegible]	[illegible]	[illegible]	[illegible]	[illegible]	[illegible]
Meath,	[illegible]	[illegible]	[illegible]	[illegible]	[illegible]	[illegible]
Queen's,	[illegible]	[illegible]	[illegible]	[illegible]	[illegible]	[illegible]
Westmeath,	[illegible]	[illegible]	[illegible]	[illegible]	[illegible]	[illegible]
Wexford,	[illegible]	[illegible]	[illegible]	[illegible]	[illegible]	[illegible]
Wicklow,	[illegible]	[illegible]	[illegible]	[illegible]	[illegible]	[illegible]
Total,	[illegible]	[illegible]	[illegible]	[illegible]	[illegible]	[illegible]
Connaught:						
Galway,	[illegible]	[illegible]	[illegible]	[illegible]	[illegible]	[illegible]
Leitrim,	[illegible]	[illegible]	[illegible]	[illegible]	[illegible]	[illegible]
Mayo,	[illegible]	[illegible]	[illegible]	[illegible]	[illegible]	[illegible]
Roscommon,	[illegible]	[illegible]	[illegible]	[illegible]	[illegible]	[illegible]
Sligo,	[illegible]	[illegible]	[illegible]	[illegible]	[illegible]	[illegible]
Total,	[illegible]	[illegible]	[illegible]	[illegible]	[illegible]	[illegible]
Munster:						
Clare,	[illegible]	[illegible]	[illegible]	[illegible]	[illegible]	[illegible]
Cork,	[illegible]	[illegible]	[illegible]	[illegible]	[illegible]	[illegible]
Kerry,	[illegible]	[illegible]	[illegible]	[illegible]	[illegible]	[illegible]
Limerick,	[illegible]	[illegible]	[illegible]	[illegible]	[illegible]	[illegible]
Tipperary,	[illegible]	[illegible]	[illegible]	[illegible]	[illegible]	[illegible]
Waterford,	[illegible]	[illegible]	[illegible]	[illegible]	[illegible]	[illegible]
Total,	[illegible]	[illegible]	[illegible]	[illegible]	[illegible]	[illegible]
Summary.						
Ulster,	[illegible]	[illegible]	[illegible]	[illegible]	[illegible]	[illegible]
Leinster,	[illegible]	[illegible]	[illegible]	[illegible]	[illegible]	[illegible]
Connaught,	[illegible]	[illegible]	[illegible]	[illegible]	[illegible]	[illegible]
Munster,	[illegible]	[illegible]	[illegible]	[illegible]	[illegible]	[illegible]
Total,	[illegible]	[illegible]	[illegible]	[illegible]	[illegible]	[illegible]

* [illegible]

XIII.—TABLE showing, according to Provinces and Counties, the Number of Cases in which Judicial Rents for Leasehold Tenancies have been fixed by Civil Bill Courts, as notified to the Irish Land Commission, during the Year ended the 21st August, 189[illegible], and also a Summary of the Acreage, Tenement Valuations, Former Rents, and Judicial Rents of the Holdings, and the Percentage of Reductions made in the Former Rents.

Province and County.	Number of Cases in which Judicial Rents have been fixed.	Area. Statute Acres.	Tenement Valuation.	Former Rent.	Judicial Rent.	Percentage of Reduction.
		a. r. p.	£ s. d.	£ s. d.	£ s. d.	
ULSTER:						
Antrim,	—	—	—	—	—	—
Armagh,	[illegible]	[illegible]	[illegible]	[illegible]	[illegible]	[illegible]
Cavan,	[illegible]	[illegible]	[illegible]	[illegible]	[illegible]	[illegible]
Donegal,	—	—	—	—	—	—
Down,	[illegible]	[illegible]	[illegible]	[illegible]	[illegible]	[illegible]
Fermanagh,	[illegible]	[illegible]	[illegible]	[illegible]	[illegible]	[illegible]
Londonderry,	[illegible]	[illegible]	[illegible]	[illegible]	[illegible]	[illegible]
Monaghan,	—	—	—	—	—	—
Tyrone,	[illegible]	[illegible]	[illegible]	[illegible]	[illegible]	[illegible]
Total,	[illegible]	[illegible]	[illegible]	[illegible]	[illegible]	[illegible]
LEINSTER:						
Carlow,	—	—	—	—	—	—
Dublin,	—	—	—	—	—	—
Kildare,	[illegible]	[illegible]	[illegible]	[illegible]	[illegible]	[illegible]
Kilkenny,	[illegible]	[illegible]	[illegible]	[illegible]	[illegible]	[illegible]
King's,	[illegible]	[illegible]	[illegible]	[illegible]	[illegible]	[illegible]
Longford,	[illegible]	[illegible]	[illegible]	[illegible]	[illegible]	[illegible]
Louth,	[illegible]	[illegible]	[illegible]	[illegible]	[illegible]	[illegible]
Meath,	[illegible]	[illegible]	[illegible]	[illegible]	[illegible]	[illegible]
Queen's,	—	—	—	—	—	—
Westmeath,	[illegible]	[illegible]	[illegible]	[illegible]	[illegible]	[illegible]
Wexford,	—	—	—	—	—	—
Wicklow,	—	—	—	—	—	—
Total,	[illegible]	[illegible]	[illegible]	[illegible]	[illegible]	[illegible]
CONNAUGHT:						
Galway,	—	—	—	—	—	—
Leitrim,	[illegible]	[illegible]	[illegible]	[illegible]	[illegible]	[illegible]
Mayo,	[illegible]	[illegible]	[illegible]	[illegible]	[illegible]	[illegible]
Roscommon,	—	—	—	—	—	—
Sligo,	—	—	—	—	—	—
Total,	[illegible]	[illegible]	[illegible]	[illegible]	[illegible]	[illegible]
MUNSTER:						
Clare,	[illegible]	[illegible]	[illegible]	[illegible]	[illegible]	[illegible]
Cork,	[illegible]	[illegible]	[illegible]	[illegible]	[illegible]	[illegible]
Kerry,	[illegible]	[illegible]	[illegible]	[illegible]	[illegible]	[illegible]
Limerick,	[illegible]	[illegible]	[illegible]	[illegible]	[illegible]	[illegible]
Tipperary,	[illegible]	[illegible]	[illegible]	[illegible]	[illegible]	[illegible]
Waterford,	[illegible]	[illegible]	[illegible]	[illegible]	[illegible]	[illegible]
Total,	[illegible]	[illegible]	[illegible]	[illegible]	[illegible]	[illegible]
SUMMARY.						
Ulster,	[illegible]	[illegible]	[illegible]	[illegible]	[illegible]	[illegible]
Leinster,	[illegible]	[illegible]	[illegible]	[illegible]	[illegible]	[illegible]
Connaught,	[illegible]	[illegible]	[illegible]	[illegible]	[illegible]	[illegible]
Munster,	[illegible]	[illegible]	[illegible]	[illegible]	[illegible]	[illegible]
Total,	[illegible]	[illegible]	[illegible]	[illegible]	[illegible]	[illegible]

XIV.—TABLE showing, according to Provinces and Counties, the Number of Cases in which Judicial Rents for Leasehold Tenancies have been fixed by Civil Bill Courts, as notified to the Irish Land Commission during the Three Years ended the 31st August, 1890, and also a Summary of the Acreage, Tenement Valuations, Former Rents, Judicial Rents of the Holdings, and the Per-centage of Reductions made in the Former Rents.

Province and County.	Number of Cases in which Judicial Rents have been fixed.	Acreage. Statute Acres.	Tenement Valuation.	Former Rent.	Judicial Rent.	Percentage of Reduction.
		A. R. P.	£ s. d.	£ s. d.	£ s. d.	
ULSTER:						
Antrim,	—	—	—	—	—	—
Armagh,	[illegible]	[illegible]	[illegible]	[illegible]	[illegible]	[illegible]
Cavan,	[illegible]	[illegible]	[illegible]	[illegible]	[illegible]	[illegible]
Donegal,	[illegible]	[illegible]	[illegible]	[illegible]	[illegible]	[illegible]
Down,	[illegible]	[illegible]	[illegible]	[illegible]	[illegible]	[illegible]
Fermanagh,	[illegible]	[illegible]	[illegible]	[illegible]	[illegible]	[illegible]
Londonderry,	[illegible]	[illegible]	[illegible]	[illegible]	[illegible]	[illegible]
Monaghan,	[illegible]	[illegible]	[illegible]	[illegible]	[illegible]	[illegible]
Tyrone,	[illegible]	[illegible]	[illegible]	[illegible]	[illegible]	[illegible]
Total,	[illegible]	[illegible]	[illegible]	[illegible]	[illegible]	[illegible]
LEINSTER:						
Carlow,	—	—	—	—	—	—
Dublin,	[illegible]	—	—	—	—	—
Kildare,	[illegible]	[illegible]	[illegible]	[illegible]	[illegible]	[illegible]
Kilkenny,	[illegible]	[illegible]	[illegible]	[illegible]	[illegible]	[illegible]
King's,	[illegible]	[illegible]	[illegible]	[illegible]	[illegible]	[illegible]
Longford,	[illegible]	[illegible]	[illegible]	[illegible]	[illegible]	[illegible]
Louth,	[illegible]	[illegible]	[illegible]	[illegible]	[illegible]	[illegible]
Meath,	[illegible]	[illegible]	[illegible]	[illegible]	[illegible]	[illegible]
Queen's,	[illegible]	[illegible]	[illegible]	[illegible]	[illegible]	—
Westmeath,	[illegible]	[illegible]	[illegible]	[illegible]	[illegible]	[illegible]
Wexford,	—	—	—	—	—	—
Wicklow,	—	—	—	—	—	—
Total,	[illegible]	[illegible]	[illegible]	[illegible]	[illegible]	[illegible]
CONNAUGHT:						
Galway,	[illegible]	[illegible]	[illegible]	[illegible]	[illegible]	[illegible]
Leitrim,	[illegible]	[illegible]	[illegible]	[illegible]	[illegible]	[illegible]
Mayo,	[illegible]	[illegible]	[illegible]	[illegible]	[illegible]	[illegible]
Roscommon,	[illegible]	[illegible]	—	[illegible]	[illegible]	[illegible]
Sligo,	—	—	—	—	—	—
Total,	[illegible]	[illegible]	[illegible]	[illegible]	[illegible]	[illegible]
MUNSTER:						
Clare,	[illegible]	[illegible]	[illegible]	[illegible]	[illegible]	[illegible]
Cork,	[illegible]	[illegible]	[illegible]	[illegible]	[illegible]	[illegible]
Kerry,	[illegible]	[illegible]	[illegible]	[illegible]	[illegible]	[illegible]
Limerick,	[illegible]	[illegible]	[illegible]	[illegible]	[illegible]	[illegible]
Tipperary,	[illegible]	[illegible]	[illegible]	[illegible]	[illegible]	[illegible]
Waterford,	[illegible]	[illegible]	[illegible]	[illegible]	[illegible]	[illegible]
Total,	[illegible]	[illegible]	[illegible]	[illegible]	[illegible]	[illegible]
SUMMARY:						
Ulster,	[illegible]	[illegible]	[illegible]	[illegible]	[illegible]	[illegible]
Leinster,	[illegible]	[illegible]	[illegible]	[illegible]	[illegible]	[illegible]
Connaught,	[illegible]	[illegible]	[illegible]	[illegible]	[illegible]	[illegible]
Munster,	[illegible]	[illegible]	[illegible]	[illegible]	[illegible]	[illegible]
Total,	[illegible]	[illegible]	[illegible]	[illegible]	[illegible]	[illegible]

AGREEMENTS FIXING FAIR RENTS.—TABLES XV. to XVIII. INCLUSIVE.

Section 8, sub-section 6, Land Law (Ireland) Act, 1881.

XV.—TABLE showing, according to Provinces and Counties, the Number of Cases in which Agreements between Landlords and Tenants fixing Fair Rents were lodged with the Land Commission during the year ended the 21st day of August, 1890, and also a Summary of the Acreage, Tenement Valuations, Former Rents, Judicial Rents of the Holdings, and the Percentage of Reduction made in the Former Rents.

Province and County.	Number of Agreements Lodged.	Acreage Statute Area.	Tenement Valuation.	Former Rent.	Judicial Rent.	Percentage of Reduction.
		a. r. p.	£ s. d.	£ s. d.	£ s. d.	
ULSTER.						
Antrim,	[illegible]	[illegible]	[illegible]	[illegible]	[illegible]	[illegible]
Armagh,	[illegible]	[illegible]	[illegible]	[illegible]	[illegible]	[illegible]
Cavan,	[illegible]	[illegible]	[illegible]	[illegible]	[illegible]	[illegible]
Donegal,	[illegible]	[illegible]	[illegible]	[illegible]	[illegible]	[illegible]
Down,	[illegible]	[illegible]	[illegible]	[illegible]	[illegible]	[illegible]
Fermanagh,	[illegible]	[illegible]	[illegible]	[illegible]	[illegible]	[illegible]
Londonderry,	[illegible]	[illegible]	[illegible]	[illegible]	[illegible]	[illegible]
Monaghan,	[illegible]	[illegible]	[illegible]	[illegible]	[illegible]	[illegible]
Tyrone,	[illegible]	[illegible]	[illegible]	[illegible]	[illegible]	[illegible]
Total,	[illegible]	[illegible]	[illegible]	[illegible]	[illegible]	[illegible]
LEINSTER.						
Carlow,	[illegible]	[illegible]	[illegible]	[illegible]	[illegible]	[illegible]
Dublin,	[illegible]	[illegible]	[illegible]	[illegible]	[illegible]	[illegible]
Kildare,	[illegible]	[illegible]	[illegible]	[illegible]	[illegible]	[illegible]
Kilkenny,	[illegible]	[illegible]	[illegible]	[illegible]	[illegible]	[illegible]
King's,	[illegible]	[illegible]	[illegible]	[illegible]	[illegible]	[illegible]
Longford,	[illegible]	[illegible]	[illegible]	[illegible]	[illegible]	[illegible]
Louth,	[illegible]	[illegible]	[illegible]	[illegible]	[illegible]	[illegible]
Meath,	[illegible]	[illegible]	[illegible]	[illegible]	[illegible]	[illegible]
Queen's,	[illegible]	[illegible]	[illegible]	[illegible]	[illegible]	[illegible]
Westmeath,	[illegible]	[illegible]	[illegible]	[illegible]	[illegible]	[illegible]
Wexford,	[illegible]	[illegible]	[illegible]	[illegible]	[illegible]	[illegible]
Wicklow,	[illegible]	[illegible]	[illegible]	[illegible]	[illegible]	[illegible]
Total,	[illegible]	[illegible]	[illegible]	[illegible]	[illegible]	[illegible]
CONNAUGHT.						
Galway,	[illegible]	[illegible]	[illegible]	[illegible]	[illegible]	[illegible]
Leitrim,	[illegible]	[illegible]	[illegible]	[illegible]	[illegible]	[illegible]
Mayo,	[illegible]	[illegible]	[illegible]	[illegible]	[illegible]	[illegible]
Roscommon,	[illegible]	[illegible]	[illegible]	[illegible]	[illegible]	[illegible]
Sligo,	[illegible]	[illegible]	[illegible]	[illegible]	[illegible]	[illegible]
Total,	[illegible]	[illegible]	[illegible]	[illegible]	[illegible]	[illegible]
MUNSTER.						
Clare,	[illegible]	[illegible]	[illegible]	[illegible]	[illegible]	[illegible]
Cork,	[illegible]	[illegible]	[illegible]	[illegible]	[illegible]	[illegible]
Kerry,	[illegible]	[illegible]	[illegible]	[illegible]	[illegible]	[illegible]
Limerick,	[illegible]	[illegible]	[illegible]	[illegible]	[illegible]	[illegible]
Tipperary,	[illegible]	[illegible]	[illegible]	[illegible]	[illegible]	[illegible]
Waterford,	[illegible]	[illegible]	[illegible]	[illegible]	[illegible]	[illegible]
Total,	[illegible]	[illegible]	[illegible]	[illegible]	[illegible]	[illegible]
SUMMARY.						
Ulster,	[illegible]	[illegible]	[illegible]	[illegible]	[illegible]	[illegible]
Leinster,	[illegible]	[illegible]	[illegible]	[illegible]	[illegible]	[illegible]
Connaught,	[illegible]	[illegible]	[illegible]	[illegible]	[illegible]	[illegible]
Munster,	[illegible]	[illegible]	[illegible]	[illegible]	[illegible]	[illegible]
Total,	[illegible]	[illegible]	[illegible]	[illegible]	[illegible]	[illegible]

XVI.—TABLE showing, according to Provinces and Counties, the number of Cases in which Agreements between Landlords and Tenants fixing Fair Rents were lodged with the Land Commission during the nine years ended the 21st August, 1890, and also a Summary of the Acreage, Tenement Valuations, Former Rents, Judicial Rents of the Holdings, and the Percentage of Reduction made in the Former Rents.

PROVINCE AND COUNTY.	Number of Agreements Lodged.	Acreage. Statute Acres.	Tenement Valuation.	Former Rent.	Judicial Rent.	Percentage of Reduction.
		a. r. p.	£ s. d.	£ s. d.	£ s. d.	
ULSTER:						
Antrim,	[illegible]	[illegible]	[illegible]	[illegible]	[illegible]	[illegible]
Armagh,	[illegible]	[illegible]	[illegible]	[illegible]	[illegible]	[illegible]
Cavan,	[illegible]	[illegible]	[illegible]	[illegible]	[illegible]	[illegible]
Donegal,	[illegible]	[illegible]	[illegible]	[illegible]	[illegible]	[illegible]
Down,	[illegible]	[illegible]	[illegible]	[illegible]	[illegible]	[illegible]
Fermanagh,	[illegible]	[illegible]	[illegible]	[illegible]	[illegible]	[illegible]
Londonderry,	[illegible]	[illegible]	[illegible]	[illegible]	[illegible]	[illegible]
Monaghan,	[illegible]	[illegible]	[illegible]	[illegible]	[illegible]	[illegible]
Tyrone,	[illegible]	[illegible]	[illegible]	[illegible]	[illegible]	[illegible]
Total,	[illegible]	[illegible]	[illegible]	[illegible]	[illegible]	[illegible]
LEINSTER:						
Carlow,	[illegible]	[illegible]	[illegible]	[illegible]	[illegible]	[illegible]
Dublin,	[illegible]	[illegible]	[illegible]	[illegible]	[illegible]	[illegible]
Kildare,	[illegible]	[illegible]	[illegible]	[illegible]	[illegible]	[illegible]
Kilkenny,	[illegible]	[illegible]	[illegible]	[illegible]	[illegible]	[illegible]
King's,	[illegible]	[illegible]	[illegible]	[illegible]	[illegible]	[illegible]
Longford,	[illegible]	[illegible]	[illegible]	[illegible]	[illegible]	[illegible]
Louth,	[illegible]	[illegible]	[illegible]	[illegible]	[illegible]	[illegible]
Meath,	[illegible]	[illegible]	[illegible]	[illegible]	[illegible]	[illegible]
Queen's,	[illegible]	[illegible]	[illegible]	[illegible]	[illegible]	[illegible]
Westmeath,	[illegible]	[illegible]	[illegible]	[illegible]	[illegible]	[illegible]
Wexford,	[illegible]	[illegible]	[illegible]	[illegible]	[illegible]	[illegible]
Wicklow,	[illegible]	[illegible]	[illegible]	[illegible]	[illegible]	[illegible]
Total,	[illegible]	[illegible]	[illegible]	[illegible]	[illegible]	[illegible]
CONNAUGHT:						
Galway,	[illegible]	[illegible]	[illegible]	[illegible]	[illegible]	[illegible]
Leitrim,	[illegible]	[illegible]	[illegible]	[illegible]	[illegible]	[illegible]
Mayo,	[illegible]	[illegible]	[illegible]	[illegible]	[illegible]	[illegible]
Roscommon,	[illegible]	[illegible]	[illegible]	[illegible]	[illegible]	[illegible]
Sligo,	[illegible]	[illegible]	[illegible]	[illegible]	[illegible]	[illegible]
Total,	[illegible]	[illegible]	[illegible]	[illegible]	[illegible]	[illegible]
MUNSTER:						
Clare,	[illegible]	[illegible]	[illegible]	[illegible]	[illegible]	[illegible]
Cork,	[illegible]	[illegible]	[illegible]	[illegible]	[illegible]	[illegible]
Kerry,	[illegible]	[illegible]	[illegible]	[illegible]	[illegible]	[illegible]
Limerick,	[illegible]	[illegible]	[illegible]	[illegible]	[illegible]	[illegible]
Tipperary,	[illegible]	[illegible]	[illegible]	[illegible]	[illegible]	[illegible]
Waterford,	[illegible]	[illegible]	[illegible]	[illegible]	[illegible]	[illegible]
Total,	[illegible]	[illegible]	[illegible]	[illegible]	[illegible]	[illegible]
SUMMARY:						
Ulster,	[illegible]	[illegible]	[illegible]	[illegible]	[illegible]	[illegible]
Leinster,	[illegible]	[illegible]	[illegible]	[illegible]	[illegible]	[illegible]
Connaught,	[illegible]	[illegible]	[illegible]	[illegible]	[illegible]	[illegible]
Munster,	[illegible]	[illegible]	[illegible]	[illegible]	[illegible]	[illegible]
Total,	[illegible]	[illegible]	[illegible]	[illegible]	[illegible]	[illegible]

XVII.—Table showing, according to Provinces and Counties, the Number of Cases in which Agreements between Landlords and Tenants Fixing Fair Rents were lodged with the Civil Bill Courts, as notified to the Irish Land Commission, during the year ended 31st August, 1890, and also a Summary of the Acreage, Tenement Valuations, Former Rents, Judicial Rents of the Holdings, and the Per-centage of Reduction made in the Former Rents.

Provinces and Counties.	Number of Agreements Lodged.	Acreage. Statute Acres.	Poor Law Valuation.	Former Rent.	Judicial Rent.	Percentage of Reduction.
		a. r. p.	£ s. d.	£ s. d.	£ s. d.	
Ulster:						
Antrim,	—	—	—	—	—	—
Armagh,	—	—	—	—	—	—
Cavan,	1	[illegible]	[illegible]	[illegible]	[illegible]	[illegible]
Donegal,	—	—	—	—	—	—
Down,	—	—	—	—	—	—
Fermanagh,	1	[illegible]	[illegible]	[illegible]	[illegible]	[illegible]
Londonderry,	—	—	—	—	—	—
Monaghan,	[illegible]	[illegible]	[illegible]	[illegible]	[illegible]	[illegible]
Tyrone,	—	—	—	—	—	—
Total,	[illegible]	[illegible]	[illegible]	[illegible]	[illegible]	[illegible]
Leinster:						
Carlow,	1	[illegible]	[illegible]	[illegible]	[illegible]	[illegible]
Dublin,	—	—	—	—	—	—
Kildare,	[illegible]	[illegible]	[illegible]	[illegible]	[illegible]	[illegible]
Kilkenny,	—	—	—	—	—	—
King's,	[illegible]	[illegible]	[illegible]	[illegible]	[illegible]	[illegible]
Longford,	[illegible]	[illegible]	[illegible]	[illegible]	[illegible]	[illegible]
Louth,	—	—	—	—	—	—
Meath,	—	—	—	—	—	—
Queen's,	1	[illegible]	—	[illegible]	[illegible]	[illegible]
Westmeath,	—	—	—	—	—	—
Wexford,	1	[illegible]	[illegible]	[illegible]	[illegible]	—
Wicklow,	1	[illegible]	[illegible]	[illegible]	[illegible]	[illegible]
Total,	[illegible]	[illegible]	[illegible]	[illegible]	[illegible]	[illegible]
Connaught:						
Galway,	—	—	—	—	—	—
Leitrim,	—	—	—	—	—	—
Mayo,	[illegible]	[illegible]	[illegible]	[illegible]	[illegible]	[illegible]
Roscommon,	—	—	—	—	—	—
Sligo,	—	—	—	—	—	—
Total,	[illegible]	[illegible]	[illegible]	[illegible]	[illegible]	[illegible]
Munster:						
Clare,	—	—	—	—	—	—
Cork,	[illegible]	[illegible]	[illegible]	[illegible]	[illegible]	[illegible]
Kerry,	1	[illegible]	[illegible]	[illegible]	[illegible]	[illegible]
Limerick,	—	—	—	—	—	—
Tipperary,	—	—	—	—	—	—
Waterford,	—	—	—	—	—	—
Total,	[illegible]	[illegible]	[illegible]	[illegible]	[illegible]	[illegible]
Summary:						
Ulster,	[illegible]	[illegible]	[illegible]	[illegible]	[illegible]	[illegible]
Leinster,	[illegible]	[illegible]	[illegible]	[illegible]	[illegible]	[illegible]
Connaught,	[illegible]	[illegible]	[illegible]	[illegible]	[illegible]	[illegible]
Munster,	[illegible]	[illegible]	[illegible]	[illegible]	[illegible]	[illegible]
Total,	[illegible]	[illegible]	[illegible]	[illegible]	[illegible]	[illegible]

XVIII.—TABLE showing, according to Provinces and Counties, the Number of Cases in which Agreements between Landlords and Tenants fixing Fair Rents were lodged with the Civil Bill Courts, as notified to the Irish Land Commission during the nine years ended the 31st day of August, 1890, and also a Summary of the Acreage, Tenement Valuations, Former Rents, Judicial Rents of the Holdings, and the Per-centage of Reduction made in the Former Rents.

Province and County.	Number of Agreements lodged.	Acreage (Statute Acres).	Poor Law Valuation.	Former Rent.	Judicial Rent.	Per-centage of Reduction.
		A. R. P.	£ s. d.	£ s. d.	£ s. d.	
ULSTER:						
Antrim,	—	—	—	—	—	—
Armagh,	[illegible]	[illegible]	[illegible]	[illegible]	[illegible]	[illegible]
Cavan,	[illegible]	[illegible]	[illegible]	[illegible]	[illegible]	[illegible]
Donegal,	[illegible]	[illegible]	[illegible]	[illegible]	[illegible]	[illegible]
Down,	[illegible]	[illegible]	[illegible]	[illegible]	[illegible]	[illegible]
Fermanagh,	[illegible]	[illegible]	[illegible]	[illegible]	[illegible]	[illegible]
Londonderry,	[illegible]	[illegible]	[illegible]	[illegible]	[illegible]	[illegible]
Monaghan,	[illegible]	[illegible]	[illegible]	[illegible]	[illegible]	[illegible]
Tyrone,	[illegible]	[illegible]	[illegible]	[illegible]	[illegible]	[illegible]
Total,	[illegible]	[illegible]	[illegible]	[illegible]	[illegible]	[illegible]
LEINSTER:						
Carlow,	[illegible]	[illegible]	[illegible]	[illegible]	[illegible]	[illegible]
Dublin,	—	—	—	—	—	—
Kildare,	[illegible]	[illegible]	[illegible]	[illegible]	[illegible]	[illegible]
Kilkenny,	[illegible]	[illegible]	[illegible]	[illegible]	[illegible]	[illegible]
King's,	[illegible]	[illegible]	[illegible]	[illegible]	[illegible]	[illegible]
Longford,	[illegible]	[illegible]	[illegible]	[illegible]	[illegible]	[illegible]
Louth,	[illegible]	[illegible]	[illegible]	[illegible]	[illegible]	[illegible]
Meath,	[illegible]	[illegible]	[illegible]	[illegible]	[illegible]	[illegible]
Queen's,	[illegible]	[illegible]	[illegible]	[illegible]	[illegible]	[illegible]
Westmeath,	[illegible]	[illegible]	[illegible]	[illegible]	[illegible]	[illegible]
Wexford,	[illegible]	[illegible]	[illegible]	[illegible]	[illegible]	[illegible]
Wicklow,	[illegible]	[illegible]	[illegible]	[illegible]	[illegible]	[illegible]
Total,	[illegible]	[illegible]	[illegible]	[illegible]	[illegible]	[illegible]
CONNAUGHT:						
Galway,	[illegible]	[illegible]	[illegible]	[illegible]	[illegible]	[illegible]
Leitrim,	[illegible]	[illegible]	[illegible]	[illegible]	[illegible]	[illegible]
Mayo,	[illegible]	[illegible]	[illegible]	[illegible]	[illegible]	[illegible]
Roscommon,	[illegible]	[illegible]	[illegible]	[illegible]	[illegible]	[illegible]
Sligo,	[illegible]	[illegible]	[illegible]	[illegible]	[illegible]	[illegible]
Total,	[illegible]	[illegible]	[illegible]	[illegible]	[illegible]	[illegible]
MUNSTER:						
Clare,	[illegible]	[illegible]	[illegible]	[illegible]	[illegible]	[illegible]
Cork,	[illegible]	[illegible]	[illegible]	[illegible]	[illegible]	[illegible]
Kerry,	[illegible]	[illegible]	[illegible]	[illegible]	[illegible]	[illegible]
Limerick,	[illegible]	[illegible]	[illegible]	[illegible]	[illegible]	[illegible]
Tipperary,	[illegible]	[illegible]	[illegible]	[illegible]	[illegible]	[illegible]
Waterford,	[illegible]	[illegible]	[illegible]	[illegible]	[illegible]	[illegible]
Total,	[illegible]	[illegible]	[illegible]	[illegible]	[illegible]	[illegible]
SUMMARY.						
Ulster,	[illegible]	[illegible]	[illegible]	[illegible]	[illegible]	[illegible]
Leinster,	[illegible]	[illegible]	[illegible]	[illegible]	[illegible]	[illegible]
Connaught,	[illegible]	[illegible]	[illegible]	[illegible]	[illegible]	[illegible]
Munster,	[illegible]	[illegible]	[illegible]	[illegible]	[illegible]	[illegible]
Total,	[illegible]	[illegible]	[illegible]	[illegible]	[illegible]	[illegible]

ARBITRATION RETURNS.—TABLES XIX. to XXVI. inclusive.

Section 40,—Land Law (Ireland) Act, 1881.

XIX.—TABLE showing, according to Provinces and Counties, the Number of Cases in which Rents have been fixed by Arbitration and the Awards recorded in the Court of the Irish Land Commission during the Year ended 31st August, 1890, with the Acreage, Tenement Valuations, Former Rents, Judicial Rents of the Holdings, and the Per-centage of Reduction made in the Former Rents.

Province and County.	Number of Cases.	Acreage (Statute Acres).	Tenement Valuation.	Former Rent.	Judicial Rent fixed by Award.	Percentage of Reduction.
ULSTER:		A. R. P.	£ s. d.	£ s. d.	£ s. d.	
Cavan,	1	[illegible]	[illegible]	[illegible]	[illegible]	[illegible]

XX.—TABLE showing, according to Provinces and Counties, the Number of Cases in which Rents have been fixed by Arbitration, and the Awards Recorded in the Court of the Irish Land Commission during the nine years ended 31st August, 1890, with the Acreage, Tenement Valuations, Former Rents, Judicial Rents of the Holdings, and the Per-centage of Reduction made in the Former Rents.

Province and County.	Number of Cases.	Acreage (Statute Acres).	Tenement Valuation.	Former Rent.	Judicial Rent fixed by Award.	Per-centage of Reduction.
ULSTER:		A. R. P.	£ s. d.	£ s. d.	£ s. d.	
Antrim,	1	[illegible]	[illegible]	[illegible]	[illegible]	[illegible]
Armagh,	1	[illegible]	[illegible]	[illegible]	[illegible]	[illegible]
Cavan,	1	[illegible]	[illegible]	[illegible]	[illegible]	[illegible]
Total,	3	[illegible]	[illegible]	[illegible]	[illegible]	[illegible]
LEINSTER:						
Meath,	[illegible]	[illegible]	[illegible]	[illegible]	[illegible]	[illegible]
CONNAUGHT:						
Roscommon,	[illegible]	[illegible]	[illegible]	[illegible]	[illegible]	[illegible]
MUNSTER:						
Cork,	[illegible]	[illegible]	[illegible]	[illegible]	[illegible]	[illegible]
Limerick,	[illegible]	[illegible]	[illegible]	[illegible]	[illegible]	[illegible]
Waterford,	[illegible]	[illegible]	[illegible]	[illegible]	[illegible]	[illegible]
Total,	[illegible]	[illegible]	[illegible]	[illegible]	[illegible]	[illegible]
SUMMARY.						
Ulster,	[illegible]	[illegible]	[illegible]	[illegible]	[illegible]	[illegible]
Leinster,	[illegible]	[illegible]	[illegible]	[illegible]	[illegible]	[illegible]
Connaught,	[illegible]	[illegible]	[illegible]	[illegible]	[illegible]	[illegible]
Munster,	[illegible]	[illegible]	[illegible]	[illegible]	[illegible]	[illegible]
Total,	[illegible]	[illegible]	[illegible]	[illegible]	[illegible]	[illegible]

XXI.—TABLE showing, according to Provinces and Counties, the Number of Submissions to Arbitration which have been lodged in the Court of the Irish Land Commission during the year ended 31st August, 1890.

Province and County.	Number of Submissions lodged.	Province and County.	Number of Submissions lodged.
ULSTER:		CONNAUGHT:	
Antrim,	[illegible]	Galway,	[illegible]
Armagh,	[illegible]	Leitrim,	[illegible]
Cavan,	[illegible]	Mayo,	[illegible]
Donegal,	[illegible]	Roscommon,	[illegible]
Down,	[illegible]	Sligo,	[illegible]
Fermanagh,	[illegible]	Total,	[illegible]
Londonderry,	[illegible]	MUNSTER:	
Monaghan,	[illegible]	Clare,	[illegible]
Tyrone,	[illegible]	Cork,	[illegible]
Total,	[illegible]	Kerry,	[illegible]
LEINSTER:		Limerick,	[illegible]
Carlow,	[illegible]	Tipperary,	[illegible]
Dublin,	[illegible]	Waterford,	[illegible]
Kildare,	[illegible]	Total,	[illegible]
Kilkenny,	[illegible]	SUMMARY:	
King's,	[illegible]	Ulster,	[illegible]
Longford,	[illegible]	Leinster,	[illegible]
Louth,	[illegible]	Connaught,	[illegible]
Meath,	[illegible]	Munster,	[illegible]
Queen's,	[illegible]	Total,	[illegible]
Westmeath,	[illegible]		
Wexford,	[illegible]		
Wicklow,	[illegible]		
Total,	[illegible]		

XXII.—TABLE showing, according to Provinces and Counties, the Number of Submissions to Arbitration which have been lodged in the Court of the Irish Land Commission during the nine years ended 21st August, 1890.

Province and County.	Number of Submissions lodged.	Province and County.	Number of Submissions lodged.
ULSTER:		CONNAUGHT:	
Antrim,	[illegible]	Galway,	[illegible]
Armagh,	[illegible]	Leitrim,	–
Cavan,	[illegible]	Mayo,	–
Donegal,	[illegible]	Roscommon,	[illegible]
Down,	[illegible]	Sligo,	[illegible]
Fermanagh,	[illegible]	Total,	[illegible]
Londonderry,	[illegible]		
Monaghan,	–		
Tyrone,	[illegible]	MUNSTER:	
Total,	[illegible]	Clare,	[illegible]
		Cork,	[illegible]
LEINSTER:		Kerry,	–
Carlow,	–	Limerick,	[illegible]
Dublin,	–	Tipperary,	[illegible]
Kildare,	–	Waterford,	[illegible]
Kilkenny,	–	Total,	[illegible]
King's,	–		
Longford,	–	SUMMARY:	
Louth,	–		
Meath,	[illegible]	Ulster,	[illegible]
Queen's,	[illegible]	Leinster,	[illegible]
Westmeath,	–	Connaught,	[illegible]
Wexford,	[illegible]	Munster,	[illegible]
Wicklow,	[illegible]		
Total,	[illegible]	TOTAL,	[illegible]

XXIII.—TABLE showing, according to Provinces and Counties, the Number of Cases in which Rents have been fixed by Arbitration and the Awards recorded in the Civil Bill Courts during the year ended 21st August, 1890, with the Average, Tenement Valuations, Former Rents, Judicial Rents of the Holdings, and the Percentage of Reduction made in the Former Rents.

Province and County.	Number of Cases.	Average Statute Acres.	Tenement Valuation.	Former Rent.	Judicial Rent fixed by Award.	Percentage of Reduction.
—	[illegible]	[illegible]	[illegible]	[illegible]	[illegible]	[illegible]

XXV.—Table showing, according to Provinces and Counties, the Number of Submissions to Arbitration which have been lodged in the Civil Bill Courts during the year ended 21st August, 18[illegible].

Province and County.	Number of Submissions.	Province and County.	Number of Submissions.
Ulster:		Connaught:	
Antrim,	[illegible]	Galway,	
Armagh,	[illegible]	Leitrim,	
Cavan,	[illegible]	Mayo,	
Donegal,	[illegible]	Roscommon,	
Down,	[illegible]	Sligo,	[illegible]
Fermanagh,	[illegible]	Total,	[illegible]
Londonderry,	[illegible]		
Monaghan,	[illegible]	Munster:	
Tyrone,	[illegible]	Clare,	
Total,	[illegible]	Cork,	
		Kerry,	[illegible]
Leinster:		Limerick,	[illegible]
Carlow,	[illegible]	Tipperary,	[illegible]
Dublin,	[illegible]	Waterford,	[illegible]
Kildare,	[illegible]	Total,	[illegible]
Kilkenny,	[illegible]		
King's,	[illegible]		
Longford,	[illegible]		
Louth,	[illegible]	Summary:	
Meath,	[illegible]	Ulster,	
Queen's,	[illegible]	Leinster,	
Westmeath,	[illegible]	Connaught,	
Wexford,	[illegible]	Munster,	
Wicklow,	[illegible]		
Total,	[illegible]	Total,	[illegible]

Province and County			
Ulster:			
Antrim,	[illegible]	[illegible]	[illegible]
Armagh,	[illegible]	[illegible]	[illegible]
Cavan,	[illegible]	[illegible]	[illegible]
Donegal,	[illegible]	[illegible]	[illegible]
Down,	[illegible]	[illegible]	[illegible]
Fermanagh,	[illegible]	[illegible]	[illegible]
Londonderry,	[illegible]	[illegible]	[illegible]
Monaghan,	[illegible]	[illegible]	[illegible]
Tyrone,	[illegible]	[illegible]	[illegible]
Total,	[illegible]	[illegible]	[illegible]
Leinster:			
Carlow,	[illegible]	[illegible]	[illegible]
Dublin,	[illegible]	[illegible]	[illegible]
Kildare,	[illegible]	[illegible]	[illegible]
Kilkenny,	[illegible]	[illegible]	[illegible]
King's,	[illegible]	[illegible]	[illegible]
Longford,	[illegible]	[illegible]	[illegible]
Louth,	[illegible]	[illegible]	[illegible]
Meath,	[illegible]	[illegible]	[illegible]
Queen's,	[illegible]	[illegible]	[illegible]
Westmeath,	[illegible]	[illegible]	[illegible]
Wexford,	[illegible]	[illegible]	[illegible]
Wicklow,	[illegible]	[illegible]	[illegible]
Total,	[illegible]	[illegible]	[illegible]

Province and County	
Connaught:	
Galway,	[illegible]
Leitrim,	[illegible]
Mayo,	[illegible]
Roscommon,	[illegible]
Sligo,	[illegible]
Total,	[illegible]
Munster:	
Clare,	[illegible]
Cork,	[illegible]
Kerry,	[illegible]
Limerick,	[illegible]
Tipperary,	[illegible]
Waterford,	[illegible]
Total,	[illegible]
SUMMARY:	
Ulster,	[illegible]
Leinster,	[illegible]
Connaught,	[illegible]
Munster,	[illegible]
Total,	[illegible]

…XVIII.—Table showing, according to Provinces and Counties, …
the hearing of Cases heard by Sub-Commissions lodged during …
1890; the Number Heard, and the Number Withdrawn.

Province and County	Number of Appeals Lodged	Number Heard	Number Withdrawn
Ulster:			
Antrim,	[illegible]	[illegible]	[illegible]
Armagh,	[illegible]	[illegible]	[illegible]
Cavan,	[illegible]	[illegible]	[illegible]
Donegal,	[illegible]	[illegible]	[illegible]
Down,	[illegible]	[illegible]	[illegible]
Fermanagh,	[illegible]	[illegible]	[illegible]
Londonderry,	[illegible]	[illegible]	[illegible]
Monaghan,	[illegible]	[illegible]	[illegible]
Tyrone,	[illegible]	[illegible]	[illegible]
Total,	[illegible]	[illegible]	[illegible]
Leinster:			
Carlow,	[illegible]	[illegible]	[illegible]
Dublin,	[illegible]	[illegible]	[illegible]
Kildare,	[illegible]	[illegible]	[illegible]
Kilkenny,	[illegible]	[illegible]	[illegible]
King's,	[illegible]	[illegible]	[illegible]
Longford,	[illegible]	[illegible]	[illegible]
Louth,	[illegible]	[illegible]	[illegible]
Meath,	[illegible]	[illegible]	[illegible]
Queen's,	[illegible]	[illegible]	[illegible]
Westmeath,	[illegible]	[illegible]	[illegible]
Wexford,	[illegible]	[illegible]	[illegible]
Wicklow,	[illegible]	[illegible]	[illegible]
Total,	[illegible]	[illegible]	[illegible]
Connaught:			
Galway,	[illegible]	[illegible]	[illegible]
Leitrim,	[illegible]	[illegible]	[illegible]
Mayo,	[illegible]	[illegible]	[illegible]
Roscommon,	1,606	[illegible]	[illegible]
Sligo,	[illegible]	[illegible]	[illegible]
Total,	[illegible]	[illegible]	[illegible]
Munster:			
Clare,	[illegible]	[illegible]	[illegible]
Cork,	[illegible]	[illegible]	[illegible]
Kerry,	[illegible]	[illegible]	[illegible]
Limerick,	[illegible]	[illegible]	[illegible]
Tipperary,	[illegible]	[illegible]	[illegible]
Waterford,	[illegible]	[illegible]	[illegible]

XXIX.—Table showing, according to Provinces and Counties, the Results of Applications for the Re-hearing of Cases heard by Sub-Commissions, during the year ended [illegible] August, [illegible], with the Former Rents, Rents as fixed by Sub-Commissions, and Rents as fixed after Re-hearing.

Province and County.	Former Rent.	Rent fixed by Sub-Commission.	Rent fixed after Re-hearing.	Difference per cent. between Sub-Commission Rent and Rent fixed after Re-hearing.
	£ s. d.	£ s. d.	£ s. d.	
Ulster:				
Antrim,	[illegible]	[illegible]	[illegible]	[illegible]
Armagh,	[illegible]	[illegible]	[illegible]	[illegible]
Cavan,	[illegible]	[illegible]	[illegible]	[illegible]
Donegal,	[illegible]	[illegible]	[illegible]	[illegible]
Down,	[illegible]	[illegible]	[illegible]	[illegible]
Fermanagh,	[illegible]	[illegible]	[illegible]	[illegible]
Londonderry,	[illegible]	[illegible]	[illegible]	[illegible]
Monaghan,	[illegible]	[illegible]	[illegible]	[illegible]
Tyrone,	[illegible]	[illegible]	[illegible]	[illegible]
Total,	[illegible]	[illegible]	[illegible]	[illegible]
Leinster:				
Carlow,	[illegible]	[illegible]	[illegible]	[illegible]
Dublin,	[illegible]	[illegible]	[illegible]	[illegible]
Kildare,	[illegible]	[illegible]	[illegible]	[illegible]
Kilkenny,	[illegible]	[illegible]	[illegible]	[illegible]
King's,	[illegible]	[illegible]	[illegible]	[illegible]
Longford,	[illegible]	[illegible]	[illegible]	[illegible]
Louth,	[illegible]	[illegible]	[illegible]	[illegible]
Meath,	[illegible]	[illegible]	[illegible]	[illegible]
Queen's,	[illegible]	[illegible]	[illegible]	[illegible]
Westmeath,	[illegible]	[illegible]	[illegible]	[illegible]
Wexford,	[illegible]	[illegible]	[illegible]	[illegible]
Wicklow,	[illegible]	[illegible]	[illegible]	[illegible]
Total,	[illegible]	[illegible]	[illegible]	[illegible]
Connaught:				
Galway,	[illegible]	[illegible]	[illegible]	[illegible]
Leitrim,	[illegible]	[illegible]	[illegible]	[illegible]
Mayo,	[illegible]	[illegible]	[illegible]	[illegible]
Roscommon,	[illegible]	[illegible]	[illegible]	[illegible]
Sligo,	[illegible]	[illegible]	[illegible]	[illegible]
Total,	[illegible]	[illegible]	[illegible]	[illegible]
Munster:				
Clare,	[illegible]	[illegible]	[illegible]	[illegible]
Cork,	[illegible]	[illegible]	[illegible]	[illegible]
Kerry,	[illegible]	[illegible]	[illegible]	[illegible]
Limerick,	[illegible]	[illegible]	[illegible]	[illegible]
Tipperary,	[illegible]	[illegible]	[illegible]	[illegible]
Waterford,	[illegible]	[illegible]	[illegible]	[illegible]
Total,	[illegible]	[illegible]	[illegible]	[illegible]
Summary:				
Ulster,	[illegible]	[illegible]	[illegible]	[illegible]
Leinster,	[illegible]	[illegible]	[illegible]	[illegible]
Connaught,	[illegible]	[illegible]	[illegible]	[illegible]
Munster,	[illegible]	[illegible]	[illegible]	[illegible]
Total,	[illegible]	[illegible]	[illegible]	[illegible]

XIX.—Table showing, according to Provinces and Counties, the Results of Applications for the Re-hearing of Cases heard by Sub-Commissions, during the nine years ended 31st August, [illegible], with the Former Rents, Rents as fixed by Sub-Commissions, and Rents as fixed after Re-hearing.

Province and County.	Former Rent.	Rent fixed by Sub-Commission.	Rent fixed after Re-hearing.	Difference per cent. between Sub-Commission Rent and Rent fixed after Re-hearing.
	£ s. d.	£ s. d.	£ s. d.	
Ulster:				
Antrim,	[illegible]	[illegible]	[illegible]	[illegible]
Armagh,	[illegible]	[illegible]	[illegible]	[illegible]
Cavan,	[illegible]	[illegible]	[illegible]	„ [illegible]
Donegal,	[illegible]	[illegible]	[illegible]	„ [illegible]
Down,	[illegible]	[illegible]	[illegible]	[illegible]
Fermanagh,	[illegible]	[illegible]	[illegible]	„ [illegible]
Londonderry,	[illegible]	[illegible]	[illegible]	„ [illegible]
Monaghan,	[illegible]	[illegible]	[illegible]	[illegible]
Tyrone,	[illegible]	[illegible]	[illegible]	„ [illegible]
Total,	[illegible]	[illegible]	[illegible]	[illegible]
Leinster:				
Carlow,	[illegible]	[illegible]	[illegible]	[illegible]
Dublin,	[illegible]	[illegible]	[illegible]	„ [illegible]
Kildare,	[illegible]	[illegible]	[illegible]	„ [illegible]
Kilkenny,	[illegible]	[illegible]	[illegible]	„ [illegible]
King's,	[illegible]	[illegible]	[illegible]	„ [illegible]
Longford,	[illegible]	[illegible]	[illegible]	„ [illegible]
Louth,	[illegible]	[illegible]	[illegible]	„ [illegible]
Meath,	[illegible]	[illegible]	[illegible]	„ [illegible]
Queen's,	[illegible]	[illegible]	[illegible]	„ [illegible]
Westmeath,	[illegible]	[illegible]	[illegible]	„ [illegible]
Wexford,	[illegible]	[illegible]	[illegible]	„ [illegible]
Wicklow,	[illegible]	[illegible]	[illegible]	„ [illegible]
Total,	[illegible]	[illegible]	[illegible]	[illegible]
Connaught:				
Galway,	[illegible]	[illegible]	[illegible]	[illegible]
Leitrim,	[illegible]	[illegible]	[illegible]	[illegible]
Mayo,	[illegible]	[illegible]	[illegible]	[illegible]
Roscommon,	[illegible]	[illegible]	[illegible]	„ [illegible]
Sligo,	[illegible]	[illegible]	[illegible]	„ [illegible]
Total,	[illegible]	[illegible]	[illegible]	[illegible]
Munster:				
Clare,	[illegible]	[illegible]	[illegible]	[illegible]
Cork,	[illegible]	[illegible]	[illegible]	„ [illegible]
Kerry,	[illegible]	[illegible]	[illegible]	„ [illegible]
Limerick,	[illegible]	[illegible]	[illegible]	„ [illegible]
Tipperary,	[illegible]	[illegible]	[illegible]	„ [illegible]
Waterford,	[illegible]	[illegible]	[illegible]	„ [illegible]
Total,	[illegible]	[illegible]	[illegible]	[illegible]
Summary.				
Ulster,	[illegible]	[illegible]	[illegible]	[illegible]
Leinster,	[illegible]	[illegible]	[illegible]	„ [illegible]
Connaught,	[illegible]	[illegible]	[illegible]	„ [illegible]
Munster,	[illegible]	[illegible]	[illegible]	[illegible]
Total,	[illegible]	[illegible]	[illegible]	[illegible]

XXXI.—Table showing, according to Provinces and Counties, the Number of Appeals from decisions of Civil Bill Courts lodged during the year ended 31st August, 1890, the Number Heard, and the Number Withdrawn.

Province and County.	Number of Appeals Lodged.	Number Heard.	Number Withdrawn.
Ulster:			
Antrim,	[illegible]	[illegible]	[illegible]
Armagh,	[illegible]	[illegible]	[illegible]
Cavan,	[illegible]	[illegible]	[illegible]
Donegal,	[illegible]	[illegible]	[illegible]
Down,	[illegible]	[illegible]	[illegible]
Fermanagh,	[illegible]	[illegible]	[illegible]
Londonderry,	[illegible]	[illegible]	[illegible]
Monaghan,	[illegible]	[illegible]	[illegible]
Tyrone,	[illegible]	[illegible]	[illegible]
Total,	[illegible]	[illegible]	[illegible]
Leinster:			
Carlow,	[illegible]	[illegible]	[illegible]
Dublin,	[illegible]	[illegible]	[illegible]
Kildare,	[illegible]	[illegible]	[illegible]
Kilkenny,	[illegible]	[illegible]	[illegible]
King's,	[illegible]	[illegible]	[illegible]
Longford,	[illegible]	[illegible]	16
Louth,	[illegible]	[illegible]	[illegible]
Meath,	[illegible]	[illegible]	[illegible]
Queen's,	[illegible]	[illegible]	[illegible]
Westmeath,	[illegible]	[illegible]	[illegible]
Wexford,	[illegible]	[illegible]	[illegible]
Wicklow,	[illegible]	[illegible]	[illegible]
Total,	[illegible]	[illegible]	[illegible]
Connaught:			
Galway,	[illegible]	[illegible]	[illegible]
Leitrim,	[illegible]	[illegible]	[illegible]
Mayo,	[illegible]	[illegible]	[illegible]
Roscommon,	[illegible]	[illegible]	[illegible]
Sligo,	[illegible]	[illegible]	[illegible]
Total,	[illegible]	[illegible]	[illegible]
Munster:			
Clare,	[illegible]	[illegible]	[illegible]
Cork,	[illegible]	[illegible]	[illegible]
Kerry,	[illegible]	[illegible]	[illegible]
Limerick,	[illegible]	[illegible]	[illegible]
Tipperary,	[illegible]	[illegible]	[illegible]
Waterford,	[illegible]	[illegible]	7
Total,	[illegible]	[illegible]	[illegible]
Summary:			
Ulster,	[illegible]	[illegible]	[illegible]
Leinster,	[illegible]	[illegible]	[illegible]
Connaught,	[illegible]	[illegible]	[illegible]
Munster,	[illegible]	[illegible]	[illegible]
Total,	[illegible]	[illegible]	[illegible]

XXXII.—Table showing, according to Provinces and Counties, the Number of Appeals from Decisions of Civil Bill Courts lodged during the nine years ended 31st August, 1890, the Number Heard, and the Number Withdrawn.

Province and County.	Number of Appeals Lodged.	Number Heard.	Number Withdrawn.	[illegible]	[illegible]
Ulster:					
Antrim,	[illegible]	[illegible]	[illegible]	[illegible]	[illegible]
Armagh,	[illegible]	[illegible]	[illegible]	[illegible]	[illegible]
Cavan,	[illegible]	[illegible]	[illegible]	[illegible]	[illegible]
Donegal,	[illegible]	[illegible]	[illegible]	[illegible]	[illegible]
Down,	[illegible]	[illegible]	[illegible]	[illegible]	[illegible]
Fermanagh,	[illegible]	[illegible]	[illegible]	[illegible]	[illegible]
Londonderry,	[illegible]	[illegible]	[illegible]	[illegible]	[illegible]
Monaghan,	[illegible]	[illegible]	[illegible]	[illegible]	[illegible]
Tyrone,	[illegible]	[illegible]	[illegible]	[illegible]	[illegible]
Total,	[illegible]	[illegible]	[illegible]	[illegible]	[illegible]
Leinster:					
Carlow,	[illegible]	[illegible]	[illegible]	[illegible]	[illegible]
Dublin,	[illegible]	[illegible]	[illegible]	[illegible]	[illegible]
Kildare,	[illegible]	[illegible]	[illegible]	[illegible]	[illegible]
Kilkenny,	[illegible]	[illegible]	[illegible]	[illegible]	[illegible]
King's,	[illegible]	[illegible]	[illegible]	[illegible]	[illegible]
Longford,	[illegible]	[illegible]	[illegible]	[illegible]	[illegible]
Louth,	[illegible]	[illegible]	[illegible]	[illegible]	[illegible]
Meath,	[illegible]	[illegible]	[illegible]	[illegible]	[illegible]
Queen's,	[illegible]	[illegible]	[illegible]	[illegible]	[illegible]
Westmeath,	[illegible]	[illegible]	[illegible]	[illegible]	[illegible]
Wexford,	[illegible]	[illegible]	[illegible]	[illegible]	[illegible]
Wicklow,	[illegible]	[illegible]	[illegible]	[illegible]	[illegible]
Total,	[illegible]	[illegible]	[illegible]	[illegible]	[illegible]
Connaught:					
Galway,	[illegible]	[illegible]	[illegible]	[illegible]	[illegible]
Leitrim,	[illegible]	[illegible]	[illegible]	[illegible]	[illegible]
Mayo,	[illegible]	[illegible]	[illegible]	[illegible]	[illegible]
Roscommon,	[illegible]	[illegible]	[illegible]	[illegible]	[illegible]
Sligo,	[illegible]	[illegible]	[illegible]	[illegible]	[illegible]
Total,	[illegible]	[illegible]	[illegible]	[illegible]	[illegible]
Munster:					
Clare,	[illegible]	[illegible]	[illegible]	[illegible]	[illegible]
Cork,	[illegible]	[illegible]	[illegible]	[illegible]	[illegible]
Kerry,	[illegible]	[illegible]	[illegible]	[illegible]	[illegible]
Limerick,	[illegible]	[illegible]	[illegible]	[illegible]	[illegible]
Tipperary,	[illegible]	[illegible]	[illegible]	[illegible]	[illegible]
Waterford,	[illegible]	[illegible]	[illegible]	[illegible]	[illegible]
Total,	[illegible]	[illegible]	[illegible]	[illegible]	[illegible]
Summary.					
Ulster,	[illegible]	[illegible]	[illegible]	[illegible]	[illegible]
Leinster,	[illegible]	[illegible]	[illegible]	[illegible]	[illegible]
Connaught,	[illegible]	[illegible]	[illegible]	[illegible]	[illegible]
Munster,	[illegible]	[illegible]	[illegible]	[illegible]	[illegible]
Total,	[illegible]	[illegible]	[illegible]	[illegible]	[illegible]

XXXIII.—Table showing, according to Provinces and Counties, the Results of Appeals from the decisions of Civil Bill Courts during the Year ended 31st August, 188[illegible], with the Former Rents, Rents as fixed by Civil Bill Courts, and the Rents as fixed on Appeal.

Province and County.	Former Rent.	Rent fixed by Civil Bill Courts.	Rent fixed on Appeal.	Difference per cent. between Civil Bill Court Rents and Rents fixed on Appeal.
Ulster:	£ s. d.	£ s. d.	£ s. d.	
Antrim,	—	—	—	—
Armagh,	[illegible]	[illegible]	[illegible]	—
Cavan,	[illegible]	[illegible]	[illegible]	[illegible]
Donegal,	—	—	—	—
Down,	—	—	—	—
Fermanagh,	[illegible]	[illegible]	[illegible]	—
Londonderry,	[illegible]	[illegible]	[illegible]	—
Monaghan,	[illegible]	[illegible]	[illegible]	[illegible]
Tyrone,	[illegible]	[illegible]	[illegible]	„ [illegible]
Total,	[illegible]	[illegible]	[illegible]	[illegible]
Leinster:				
Carlow,	—	—	—	—
Dublin,	—	—	—	—
Kildare,	—	—	—	—
Kilkenny,	—	—	—	—
King's,	[illegible]	[illegible]	[illegible]	—
Longford,	[illegible]	[illegible]	[illegible]	[illegible]
Louth,	—	—	—	—
Meath,	[illegible]	[illegible]	[illegible]	[illegible]
Queen's,	[illegible]	[illegible]	[illegible]	„ [illegible]
Westmeath,	[illegible]	[illegible]	[illegible]	[illegible]
Wexford,	—	—	—	—
Wicklow,	[illegible]	[illegible]	[illegible]	—
Total,	[illegible]	[illegible]	[illegible]	[illegible]
Connaught:				
Galway,	—	—	—	—
Leitrim,	[illegible]	[illegible]	[illegible]	[illegible]
Mayo,	—	—	—	—
Roscommon,	—	—	—	—
Sligo,	—	—	—	—
Total,	[illegible]	[illegible]	[illegible]	[illegible]
Munster:				
Clare,	—	—	—	—
Cork,	[illegible]	[illegible]	[illegible]	[illegible]
Kerry,	[illegible]	[illegible]	[illegible]	„ [illegible]
Limerick,	—	—	—	—
Tipperary,	[illegible]	[illegible]	[illegible]	—
Waterford,	[illegible]	[illegible]	[illegible]	[illegible]
Total,	[illegible]	[illegible]	[illegible]	[illegible]
Summary:				
Ulster,	[illegible]	[illegible]	[illegible]	[illegible]
Leinster,	[illegible]	[illegible]	[illegible]	„ [illegible]
Connaught,	[illegible]	[illegible]	[illegible]	„ [illegible]
Munster,	[illegible]	[illegible]	[illegible]	„ [illegible]
Total,	[illegible]	[illegible]	[illegible]	[illegible]

XXXIV.—TABLE showing, according to Provinces and Counties, the Results of Appeals from the Decisions of Civil Bill Courts during the nine years ended 21st August, 1890, with the Former Rents, Rents as fixed by Civil Bill Courts, and Rents as fixed on Appeal.

Provinces and Counties.	Former Rent.	Rent fixed by Civil Bill Courts.	Rent fixed on Appeal.	Difference per cent. between Civil Bill Court Rent and Rent fixed on Appeal.
	£ s. d.	£ s. d.	£ s. d.	
ULSTER:				
Antrim,	—	—	—	—
Armagh,	[illegible]	[illegible]	[illegible]	—
Cavan,	[illegible]	[illegible]	[illegible]	[illegible]
Donegal,	[illegible]	[illegible]	[illegible]	[illegible]
Down,	—	—	—	—
Fermanagh,	[illegible]	[illegible]	[illegible]	[illegible]
Londonderry,	[illegible]	[illegible]	[illegible]	[illegible]
Monaghan,	[illegible]	[illegible]	[illegible]	[illegible]
Tyrone,	[illegible]	[illegible]	[illegible]	[illegible]
Total,	[illegible]	[illegible]	[illegible]	[illegible]
LEINSTER:				
Carlow,	—	—	—	—
Dublin,	[illegible]	[illegible]	[illegible]	[illegible]
Kildare,	[illegible]	[illegible]	[illegible]	[illegible]
Kilkenny,	[illegible]	[illegible]	[illegible]	[illegible]
King's,	[illegible]	[illegible]	[illegible]	[illegible]
Longford,	[illegible]	[illegible]	[illegible]	[illegible]
Louth,	—	—	—	—
Meath,	[illegible]	[illegible]	[illegible]	[illegible]
Queen's,	[illegible]	[illegible]	[illegible]	[illegible]
Westmeath,	[illegible]	[illegible]	[illegible]	[illegible]
Wexford,	—	—	—	—
Wicklow,	[illegible]	[illegible]	[illegible]	—
Total,	[illegible]	[illegible]	[illegible]	[illegible]
CONNAUGHT:				
Galway,	—	—	—	—
Leitrim,	[illegible]	[illegible]	[illegible]	[illegible]
Mayo,	[illegible]	[illegible]	[illegible]	[illegible]
Roscommon,	[illegible]	[illegible]	[illegible]	[illegible]
Sligo,	[illegible]	[illegible]	[illegible]	[illegible]
Total,	[illegible]	[illegible]	[illegible]	[illegible]
MUNSTER:				
Clare,	[illegible]	[illegible]	[illegible]	[illegible]
Cork,	[illegible]	[illegible]	[illegible]	[illegible]
Kerry,	[illegible]	[illegible]	[illegible]	[illegible]
Limerick,	[illegible]	[illegible]	[illegible]	[illegible]
Tipperary,	[illegible]	[illegible]	[illegible]	[illegible]
Waterford,	[illegible]	[illegible]	[illegible]	[illegible]
Total,	[illegible]	[illegible]	[illegible]	[illegible]
SUMMARY:				
Ulster,	[illegible]	[illegible]	[illegible]	[illegible]
Leinster,	[illegible]	[illegible]	[illegible]	[illegible]
Connaught,	[illegible]	[illegible]	[illegible]	[illegible]
Munster,	[illegible]	[illegible]	[illegible]	[illegible]
Total,	[illegible]	[illegible]	[illegible]	[illegible]

LABOURERS' COTTAGES, &c.—TABLES XXXVII. AND XXXVIII.

Section 19.—Land Law (Ireland) Act, 1881.

XXXVII.—TABLE showing, according to Provinces and Counties, the Number of Cases in which Orders have been made by Sub-Commissions respecting Labourers' Cottages and Allotments during the Year ended the 21st August, 1890.

Province and County.	Number of Cases.	Province and County.	Number of Cases.
ULSTER:		CONNAUGHT:	
Antrim,	–	Galway,	–
Armagh,	–	Leitrim,	–
Cavan,	–	Mayo,	–
Donegal,	–	Roscommon,	–
Down,	–	Sligo,	–
Fermanagh,	–	Total,	–
Londonderry,	–		
Monaghan,	–	MUNSTER:	
Tyrone,	–	Clare,	1
Total,	–	Cork,	1
		Kerry,	–
LEINSTER:		Limerick,	–
Carlow,	–	Tipperary,	–
Dublin,	1	Waterford,	–
Kildare,	–	Total,	[illegible]
Kilkenny,	–		
King's,	–	SUMMARY:	
Longford,	–	Ulster,	–
Louth,	–	Leinster,	[illegible]
Meath,	–	Connaught,	–
Queen's,	–	Munster,	[illegible]
Westmeath,	–	Total,	[illegible]
Wexford,	–		
Wicklow,	[illegible]		
Total,	[illegible]		

XXXVIII.—TABLE showing, according to Provinces and Counties, the Number of Cases in which Orders have been made by Sub-Commissions respecting Labourers' Cottages and Allotments during the nine years ended 21st August, 1890.

Province and County.	Number of Cases.	Province and County.	Number of Cases.
ULSTER:		CONNAUGHT:	
Antrim,	[illegible]	Galway,	[illegible]
Armagh,	[illegible]	Leitrim,	[illegible]
Cavan,	[illegible]	Mayo,	[illegible]
Donegal,	[illegible]	Roscommon,	[illegible]
Down,	[illegible]	Sligo,	[illegible]
Fermanagh,	[illegible]	Total,	[illegible]
Londonderry,	[illegible]		
Monaghan,	[illegible]	MUNSTER:	
Tyrone,	[illegible]	Clare,	[illegible]
Total,	[illegible]	Cork,	[illegible]
		Kerry,	[illegible]
LEINSTER:		Limerick,	[illegible]
Carlow,	[illegible]	Tipperary,	[illegible]
Dublin,	[illegible]	Waterford,	[illegible]
Kildare,	[illegible]	Total,	[illegible]
Kilkenny,	[illegible]		
King's,	[illegible]	SUMMARY.	
Longford,	[illegible]	Ulster,	[illegible]
Louth,	[illegible]	Leinster,	[illegible]
Meath,	[illegible]	Connaught,	[illegible]
Queen's,	[illegible]	Munster,	[illegible]
Westmeath,	[illegible]	Total,	[illegible]
Wexford,	[illegible]		
Wicklow,	[illegible]		
Total,	[illegible]		

JUDICIAL LEASES.—TABLES XXXIX. TO XLII. INCLUSIVE.

Section 10.—Land Law (Ireland) Act, 1881.

XXXIX.—TABLE showing the Number of Applications to the Land Commission to sanction Judicial Leases Received, with the Number Sealed, during the year ended 31st August, 1890.

PROVINCES AND COUNTIES.	Number of Applications received.	Number of Leases sealed.
LEINSTER:		
Carlow,	[illegible]	[illegible]
Dublin,	[illegible]	–
Total,	[illegible]	[illegible]
CONNAUGHT:		
Roscommon,	[illegible]	[illegible]
Total,	[illegible]	[illegible]
MUNSTER:		
Limerick,	[illegible]	–
Total,	[illegible]	–
SUMMARY.		
Leinster,	[illegible]	[illegible]
Connaught,	[illegible]	[illegible]
Munster,	[illegible]	–
Total,	[illegible]	[illegible]

XL.—TABLE showing the Number of Applications to the Land Commission to sanction Judicial Leases Received, with the Number Sealed, during the nine years ended 31st August, 1890.

PROVINCES AND COUNTIES.	Number of Applications received.	Number of Leases sealed.
ULSTER:		
Antrim,	[illegible]	[illegible]
Cavan,	[illegible]	[illegible]
Tyrone,	[illegible]	[illegible]
Total,	[illegible]	[illegible]
LEINSTER:		
Carlow,	[illegible]	[illegible]
Dublin,	[illegible]	[illegible]
Kildare,	[illegible]	[illegible]
Kilkenny,	[illegible]	[illegible]
King's,	[illegible]	[illegible]
Longford,	[illegible]	[illegible]
Louth,	[illegible]	[illegible]
Meath,	[illegible]	[illegible]
Queen's,	[illegible]	[illegible]
Westmeath,	[illegible]	[illegible]
Wexford,	[illegible]	[illegible]
Wicklow,	[illegible]	[illegible]
Total,	[illegible]	[illegible]
CONNAUGHT:		
Roscommon,	[illegible]	[illegible]
Total,	[illegible]	[illegible]
MUNSTER:		
Clare,	[illegible]	[illegible]
Cork,	[illegible]	[illegible]
Kerry,	[illegible]	[illegible]
Limerick,	[illegible]	[illegible]
Tipperary,	[illegible]	[illegible]
Waterford,	[illegible]	[illegible]
Total,	[illegible]	[illegible]

XLI.—TABLE showing the Number of Applications to the Civil Bill Courts to sanction Judicial Leases Received, with the Number Sealed, during the year ended 31st August, 1890.

Province and County.	Number of Applications received.	Number of Leases sealed.
Nil.	Nil.	Nil.

XLII.—TABLE showing the Number of Applications to the Civil Bill Courts to sanction Judicial Leases Received, with the Number Sealed, during the nine years ended 31st August, 1890.

Province and County.	Number of Applications received.	Number of Leases sealed.	Dismissed or struck out.
ULSTER:			
Antrim, . . .	19	—	—
Total, . . .	19	—	—
LEINSTER:			
Kildare, . . .	4	—	—
King's, . . .	5	—	—
Total, . . .	9	—	—
MUNSTER:			
Cork, ...	21	1	—
Kerry, ...	1	—	—
Limerick, . . .	1	1	—
Tipperary, . . .	2	—	2
Waterford, . . .	1	1	—
Total, . . .	26	3	2
SUMMARY.			
Ulster, . . .	19	—	—
Leinster, . . .	9	—	—
Munster, . . .	26	3	2
Total, . . .	54	3	2

FIXED TENANCIES.—TABLES XLIII. TO XLVI. INCLUSIVE.

Section 11.—Land Law (Ireland) Act, 1881.

XLIII.—TABLE showing the Number of Applications to the Land Commission to sanction Fixed Tenancies Received, with the Number Sealed, during the year ended 31st August, 1890.

Province and County.	Number of Applications received.	Number sealed.
ULSTER:		
Londonderry, . .	1	—
LEINSTER:		
King's, ...	8	—
MUNSTER:		
Tipperary, . . .	—	2
SUMMARY.		
Ulster, . . .	1	—
Leinster, . . .	8	—
Munster, . . .	—	2
Total, . . .	9	2

XLIV.—TABLE showing the Number of Applications to the Land Commission to sanction Fixed Tenancies Received, with the Number Sealed, during the nine years ended 21st August, 1890.

Province and County.	Number of Applications Received.	Number sealed.	Province and County.	Number of Applications Received.	Number sealed.
ULSTER:			MUNSTER:		
Armagh,	7	5	Cork,	9	3
Down,	5	–	Limerick,	4	2
Londonderry,	4	–	Tipperary,	13	10
Tyrone,	2	2	Total,	26	15
Total,	18	7			
LEINSTER:					
Kildare,	3	1			
King's,	3	–			
Louth,	3	1			
Wicklow,	7	–	SUMMARY.		
Total,	16	2			
CONNAUGHT:			Ulster,	18	7
Galway,	1	1	Leinster,	16	2
Roscommon,	1	–	Connaught,	3	1
Sligo,	1	–	Munster,	26	15
Total,	3	1	Total,	63	25

XLV.—TABLE showing the Number of Applications to the Civil Bill Courts to sanction Fixed Tenancies Received, with the Number Sealed, during the year ended 21st August, 1890.

Province and County.	Number of Applications received.	Number sealed.
ULSTER:		
Antrim,	1	—

XLVI.—TABLE showing the Number of Applications to the Civil Bill Courts to sanction Fixed Tenancies Received, with the Number Sealed, during the nine years ended 21st August, 1890.

Province and County.	Number of Applications received.	Number sealed.
ULSTER:		
Antrim,	3	—
Donegal,	1	—
Total,	4	—
SUMMARY.		
Ulster,	4	—
Total,	4	—

Total effect of the Land Law (Ireland) Acts, 1881 and 1887, on the Rental of Ireland.

XLVII.—TABLE showing, according to Provinces and Counties, the Number of Cases in which Judicial Rents have been fixed by all the Methods provided by the Land Law (Ireland) Acts, 1881 and 1887, during the nine years ended the 21st August, 1890; and also a Summary of the Acreage, Tenement Valuations, Former Rents, and Judicial Rents of the Holdings, and the Percentages of Reduction made in the Former Rents.

Province and County.	Number of Cases in which Judicial Rents have been fixed.	Acreage, Statute Measure.	Tenement Valuation.	Former Rent.	Judicial Rent.	Percentage of Reduction.
		A. R. P.	£ s. d.	£ s. d.	£ s. d.	
ULSTER:						
Antrim,	[illegible]	[illegible]	[illegible]	[illegible]	[illegible]	[illegible]
Armagh,	[illegible]	[illegible]	[illegible]	[illegible]	[illegible]	[illegible]
Cavan,	[illegible]	[illegible]	[illegible]	[illegible]	[illegible]	[illegible]
Donegal,	[illegible]	[illegible]	[illegible]	[illegible]	[illegible]	[illegible]
Down,	[illegible]	[illegible]	[illegible]	[illegible]	[illegible]	[illegible]
Fermanagh,	[illegible]	[illegible]	[illegible]	[illegible]	[illegible]	[illegible]
Londonderry,	[illegible]	[illegible]	[illegible]	[illegible]	[illegible]	[illegible]
Monaghan,	[illegible]	[illegible]	[illegible]	[illegible]	[illegible]	[illegible]
Tyrone,	[illegible]	[illegible]	[illegible]	[illegible]	[illegible]	[illegible]
Total,	[illegible]	[illegible]	[illegible]	[illegible]	[illegible]	[illegible]
LEINSTER:						
Carlow,	[illegible]	[illegible]	[illegible]	[illegible]	[illegible]	[illegible]
Dublin,	[illegible]	[illegible]	[illegible]	[illegible]	[illegible]	[illegible]
Kildare,	[illegible]	[illegible]	[illegible]	[illegible]	[illegible]	[illegible]
Kilkenny,	[illegible]	[illegible]	[illegible]	[illegible]	[illegible]	[illegible]
King's,	[illegible]	[illegible]	[illegible]	[illegible]	[illegible]	[illegible]
Longford,	[illegible]	[illegible]	[illegible]	[illegible]	[illegible]	[illegible]
Louth,	[illegible]	[illegible]	[illegible]	[illegible]	[illegible]	[illegible]
Meath,	[illegible]	[illegible]	[illegible]	[illegible]	[illegible]	[illegible]
Queen's,	[illegible]	[illegible]	[illegible]	[illegible]	[illegible]	[illegible]
Westmeath,	[illegible]	[illegible]	[illegible]	[illegible]	[illegible]	[illegible]
Wexford,	[illegible]	[illegible]	[illegible]	[illegible]	[illegible]	[illegible]
Wicklow,	[illegible]	[illegible]	[illegible]	[illegible]	[illegible]	[illegible]
Total,	[illegible]	[illegible]	[illegible]	[illegible]	[illegible]	[illegible]
CONNAUGHT:						
Galway,	[illegible]	[illegible]	[illegible]	[illegible]	[illegible]	[illegible]
Leitrim,	[illegible]	[illegible]	[illegible]	[illegible]	[illegible]	[illegible]
Mayo,	[illegible]	[illegible]	[illegible]	[illegible]	[illegible]	[illegible]
Roscommon,	[illegible]	[illegible]	[illegible]	[illegible]	[illegible]	[illegible]
Sligo,	[illegible]	[illegible]	[illegible]	[illegible]	[illegible]	[illegible]
Total,	[illegible]	[illegible]	[illegible]	[illegible]	[illegible]	[illegible]
MUNSTER:						
Clare,	[illegible]	[illegible]	[illegible]	[illegible]	[illegible]	[illegible]
Cork,	[illegible]	[illegible]	[illegible]	[illegible]	[illegible]	[illegible]
Kerry,	[illegible]	[illegible]	[illegible]	[illegible]	[illegible]	[illegible]
Limerick,	[illegible]	[illegible]	[illegible]	[illegible]	[illegible]	[illegible]
Tipperary,	[illegible]	[illegible]	[illegible]	[illegible]	[illegible]	[illegible]
Waterford,	[illegible]	[illegible]	[illegible]	[illegible]	[illegible]	[illegible]
Total,	[illegible]	[illegible]	[illegible]	[illegible]	[illegible]	[illegible]
SUMMARY.						
Ulster,	[illegible]	[illegible]	[illegible]	[illegible]	[illegible]	[illegible]
Leinster,	[illegible]	[illegible]	[illegible]	[illegible]	[illegible]	[illegible]
Connaught,	[illegible]	[illegible]	[illegible]	[illegible]	[illegible]	[illegible]
Munster,	[illegible]	[illegible]	[illegible]	[illegible]	[illegible]	[illegible]
Total,	[illegible]	[illegible]	[illegible]	[illegible]	[illegible]	[illegible]

[illegible]

Declaring Leases Void.—Tables XLVIII. and XLIX. inclusive.

*Section 21.—Land Law (Ireland) Act, 1881.**

XLVIII.—Table showing the Number of Applications to the Land Commission to declare Leases void received with the number disposed of during the Seven Years ended 31st August, 1888.

Provinces and Counties.	Number of Applications received.	Number of Leases declared void.	Number of Applications Dismissed, or struck out.	Number of Applications Withdrawn or compromised.	Number of Applications pending.
Ulster:					
Antrim,	[illegible]	[illegible]	[illegible]	[illegible]	.
Armagh,	[illegible]	[illegible]	[illegible]	.	.
Cavan,	[illegible]	.	[illegible]	[illegible]	.
Donegal,	[illegible]	.	[illegible]	.	.
Down,	[illegible]	.	[illegible]	[illegible]	.
Fermanagh,	[illegible]	.	[illegible]	[illegible]	.
Londonderry,	[illegible]	.	[illegible]	[illegible]	.
Monaghan,	[illegible]	.	[illegible]	.	.
Tyrone,	[illegible]	.	[illegible]	[illegible]	.
Total,	[illegible]	[illegible]	[illegible]	[illegible]	.
Leinster:					
Carlow,	[illegible]	[illegible]	[illegible]	[illegible]	.
Dublin,	[illegible]	[illegible]	[illegible]	[illegible]	.
Kildare,	[illegible]	[illegible]	[illegible]	[illegible]	.
Kilkenny,	[illegible]	.	[illegible]	[illegible]	.
King's,	[illegible]	.	[illegible]	[illegible]	.
Longford,	[illegible]	.	[illegible]	[illegible]	.
Louth,	[illegible]	[illegible]	[illegible]	[illegible]	.
Meath,	[illegible]	[illegible]	[illegible]	[illegible]	.
Queen's,	[illegible]	.	[illegible]	[illegible]	.
Westmeath,	[illegible]	.	[illegible]	[illegible]	
Wexford,	[illegible]	[illegible]	[illegible]	[illegible]	
Wicklow,	[illegible]	.	[illegible]	[illegible]	[illegible]
Total,	[illegible]	[illegible]	[illegible]	[illegible]	.
Connaught:					
Galway,	[illegible]	[illegible]	[illegible]	[illegible]	[illegible]
Leitrim,	[illegible]	[illegible]	[illegible]	[illegible]	
Mayo,	[illegible]	.	[illegible]	.	
Roscommon,	[illegible]	.	[illegible]	[illegible]	.
Sligo,	[illegible]	[illegible]	[illegible]	[illegible]	.
Total,	[illegible]	[illegible]	[illegible]	[illegible]	.
Munster:					
Clare,	[illegible]	[illegible]	[illegible]	[illegible]	.
Cork,	[illegible]	[illegible]	[illegible]	[illegible]	.
Kerry,	[illegible]	[illegible]	[illegible]	[illegible]	.
Limerick,	[illegible]	[illegible]	[illegible]	[illegible]	.
Tipperary,	[illegible]	.	[illegible]	[illegible]	.
Waterford,	[illegible]	[illegible]	[illegible]	[illegible]	.
Total,	[illegible]	[illegible]	[illegible]	[illegible]	.
Total for Ireland,	[illegible]	[illegible]	[illegible]	[illegible]	.

* The time for receiving applications under this section expired in February, [illegible].

XLIX.—TABLE showing number of applications to the Civil Bill Courts to declare Leases void, received with the number disposed of during the seven years ended 21st August, 1888.*

Province and County.	Number of applications entered.	Number of Leases declared void.	Number of applications dismissed or struck out.	Number of applications withdrawn or compromised.	Number of applications pending.
Ulster:					
Tyrone,	2	—	2	—	—
Leinster:					
Kilkenny,	1	—	—	1	—
Connaught:					
Mayo,	14	—	2	12	—
Munster:					
Waterford,	6	4	—	2	—
SUMMARY.					
Ulster,	2	—	2	—	—
Leinster,	1	—	—	1	—
Connaught,	14	—	2	12	—
Munster,	6	4	—	2	—
Total,	23	4	4	15	—

* See Note to Table XLVIII.

LAND SALES.—TABLES L. TO LIX. INCLUSIVE.

PROCEEDINGS UNDER LAND LAW (IRELAND) ACT, 1881.—TABLES L. AND LI.

L.—TABLE showing the amount of Advances applied for under Sections 24, 26 and 25 by Tenants desiring to purchase their Holdings, also the amount sanctioned and the amount advanced, during the four years ended 21st August, 1886.

Amount of advances applied for under sections 24 & 25,	£495,416
Amount sanctioned under sections 24 & 25,	358,387
Amount issued to purchasing tenants under sections 24 & 25,	195,510
Amount applied for under section 26,	51,880
Amount issued under section 26,	45,788
Total applied for under Purchase Clauses,	543,296
Total amount sanctioned,	403,915
Total amount issued,	240,294
Number of tenants who obtained advances and purchased their farms by means of such advances,	731

II.—Table showing, according to Provinces and Counties, the Amount of Advances made to Tenants under Sections 24 and 25 and Section 26 during the four years ended 21st August, 1885.

Province and County.	Under Sections 24 and 25.		Under Section 26.	
	No. of Tenants.	Amount.	No. of Tenants.	Amount.
Ulster:		£		£
Antrim,	[illegible]	[illegible]	[illegible]	[illegible]
Cavan,	[illegible]	[illegible]	[illegible]	[illegible]
Down,	[illegible]	[illegible]	[illegible]	[illegible]
Fermanagh,	[illegible]	[illegible]	—	—
Londonderry,	[illegible]	[illegible]	—	—
Monaghan,	[illegible]	[illegible]	—	—
Tyrone,	[illegible]	[illegible]	—	—
Total,	[illegible]	[illegible]	[illegible]	[illegible]
Leinster:				
Carlow,	[illegible]	[illegible]	—	—
Dublin,	[illegible]	[illegible]	—	—
Kildare,	[illegible]	[illegible]	—	—
Kilkenny,	[illegible]	[illegible]	—	—
King's,	[illegible]	[illegible]	—	—
Longford,	[illegible]	[illegible]	—	—
Louth,	[illegible]	[illegible]	—	—
Meath,	[illegible]	[illegible]	[illegible]	[illegible]
Queen's,	[illegible]	[illegible]	—	—
Westmeath,	[illegible]	[illegible]	—	—
Wexford,	[illegible]	[illegible]	—	—
Wicklow,	[illegible]	[illegible]	[illegible]	[illegible]
Total,	[illegible]	[illegible]	[illegible]	[illegible]
Connaught:				
Galway,	[illegible]	[illegible]	—	—
Leitrim,	[illegible]	[illegible]	—	—
Mayo,	[illegible]	[illegible]	[illegible]	[illegible]
Roscommon,	[illegible]	[illegible]	[illegible]	[illegible]
Sligo,	[illegible]	[illegible]	—	—
Total,	[illegible]	[illegible]	[illegible]	[illegible]
Munster:				
Cork,	[illegible]	[illegible]	—	—
Limerick,	[illegible]	[illegible]	—	—
Tipperary,	[illegible]	[illegible]	—	—
Waterford,	[illegible]	[illegible]	—	—
Total,	[illegible]	[illegible]	—	—
Summary.				
Ulster,	[illegible]	[illegible]	[illegible]	[illegible]
Leinster,	[illegible]	[illegible]	[illegible]	[illegible]
Connaught,	[illegible]	[illegible]	[illegible]	[illegible]
Munster,	[illegible]	[illegible]	—	—
Total,	[illegible]	[illegible]	[illegible]	[illegible]

N.B.—The subsequent proceedings were carried out under the Purchase of Land (Ireland) Act, 1885.

PROCEEDINGS UNDER PURCHASE OF LAND (IRELAND) ACT, 1885.—TABLES LII. TO LIX. INCLUSIVE.

LII.—RETURN showing, according to Provinces and Counties, the Number of Loans applied for, the Number of Estates, and the Total Acreage, Tenement Valuation, and Rental of the holdings embraced in the applications, also the Total Purchase-money agreed upon, and the Amount of Loans applied for, during year ended 31st August, 1890.

PROVINCES AND COUNTY.	Number of Loans. (a)	Number of Estates affected by Applications.	Acreage in Statute Measure.	Tenement Valuation. (b)	Rent. (c)	Purchase-money agreed upon.	Amount of Loans applied for.
			a. r. p.	£ s. d.	£ s. d.	£	£
ULSTER:							
Antrim,	[illegible]	[illegible]	[illegible]	[illegible]	[illegible]	[illegible]	[illegible]
Armagh,	[illegible]	[illegible]	[illegible]	[illegible]	[illegible]	[illegible]	[illegible]
Cavan,	[illegible]	[illegible]	[illegible]	[illegible]	[illegible]	[illegible]	[illegible]
Donegal,	[illegible]	[illegible]	[illegible]	[illegible]	[illegible]	[illegible]	[illegible]
Down,	[illegible]	[illegible]	[illegible]	[illegible]	[illegible]	[illegible]	[illegible]
Fermanagh,	[illegible]	[illegible]	[illegible]	[illegible]	[illegible]	[illegible]	[illegible]
Londonderry,	[illegible]	[illegible]	[illegible]	[illegible]	[illegible]	[illegible]	[illegible]
Monaghan,	[illegible]	[illegible]	[illegible]	[illegible]	[illegible]	[illegible]	[illegible]
Tyrone,	[illegible]	[illegible]	[illegible]	[illegible]	[illegible]	[illegible]	[illegible]
Total,	[illegible]	[illegible]	[illegible]	[illegible]	[illegible]	[illegible]	[illegible]
LEINSTER:							
Carlow,	[illegible]	[illegible]	[illegible]	[illegible]	[illegible]	[illegible]	[illegible]
Dublin,	[illegible]	[illegible]	[illegible]	[illegible]	[illegible]	[illegible]	[illegible]
Kildare,	[illegible]	[illegible]	[illegible]	[illegible]	[illegible]	[illegible]	[illegible]
Kilkenny,	[illegible]	[illegible]	[illegible]	[illegible]	[illegible]	[illegible]	[illegible]
King's,	[illegible]	[illegible]	[illegible]	[illegible]	[illegible]	[illegible]	[illegible]
Longford,	[illegible]	[illegible]	[illegible]	[illegible]	[illegible]	[illegible]	[illegible]
Louth,	[illegible]	[illegible]	[illegible]	[illegible]	[illegible]	[illegible]	[illegible]
Meath,	[illegible]	[illegible]	[illegible]	[illegible]	[illegible]	[illegible]	[illegible]
Queen's,	[illegible]	[illegible]	[illegible]	[illegible]	[illegible]	[illegible]	[illegible]
Westmeath,	[illegible]	[illegible]	[illegible]	[illegible]	[illegible]	[illegible]	[illegible]
Wexford,	[illegible]	[illegible]	[illegible]	[illegible]	[illegible]	[illegible]	[illegible]
Wicklow,	[illegible]	[illegible]	[illegible]	[illegible]	[illegible]	[illegible]	[illegible]
Total,	[illegible]	[illegible]	[illegible]	[illegible]	[illegible]	[illegible]	[illegible]
CONNAUGHT:							
Galway,	[illegible]	[illegible]	[illegible]	[illegible]	[illegible]	[illegible]	[illegible]
Leitrim,	[illegible]	[illegible]	[illegible]	[illegible]	[illegible]	[illegible]	[illegible]
Mayo,	[illegible]	[illegible]	[illegible]	[illegible]	[illegible]	[illegible]	[illegible]
Roscommon,	[illegible]	[illegible]	[illegible]	[illegible]	[illegible]	[illegible]	[illegible]
Sligo,	[illegible]	[illegible]	[illegible]	[illegible]	[illegible]	[illegible]	[illegible]
Total,	[illegible]	[illegible]	[illegible]	[illegible]	[illegible]	[illegible]	[illegible]
MUNSTER:							
Clare,	[illegible]	[illegible]	[illegible]	[illegible]	[illegible]	[illegible]	[illegible]
Cork,	[illegible]	[illegible]	[illegible]	[illegible]	[illegible]	[illegible]	[illegible]
Kerry,	[illegible]	[illegible]	[illegible]	[illegible]	[illegible]	[illegible]	[illegible]
Limerick,	[illegible]	[illegible]	[illegible]	[illegible]	[illegible]	[illegible]	[illegible]
Tipperary,	[illegible]	[illegible]	[illegible]	[illegible]	[illegible]	[illegible]	[illegible]
Waterford,	[illegible]	[illegible]	[illegible]	[illegible]	[illegible]	[illegible]	[illegible]
Total,	[illegible]	[illegible]	[illegible]	[illegible]	[illegible]	[illegible]	[illegible]
SUMMARY.							
Ulster,	[illegible]	[illegible]	[illegible]	[illegible]	[illegible]	[illegible]	[illegible]
Leinster,	[illegible]	[illegible]	[illegible]	[illegible]	[illegible]	[illegible]	[illegible]
Connaught,	[illegible]	[illegible]	[illegible]	[illegible]	[illegible]	[illegible]	[illegible]
Munster,	[illegible]	[illegible]	[illegible]	[illegible]	[illegible]	[illegible]	[illegible]
Total,	[illegible]	[illegible]	[illegible]	[illegible]	[illegible]	[illegible]	[illegible]

(a) The number of Tenants is the same as the number of Loans.

(b) [illegible]

(c) [illegible]

LIII.—Return showing, according to Provinces and Counties, the Number of Loans applied for, the Number of Estates, and the Total Acreage, Tenement Valuation, and Rental of the holdings embraced in the applications, also the Total Purchase-money agreed upon, and the Amount of Loans applied for, during five years ended 31st August, 18[illegible].

Province and County.	Number of Loans. (a)	Number of Estates comprised in Applications.	Acreage in Statute Measure.	Tenement Valuation. (b)	Rent. (c)	Purchase-money agreed upon.	Amount of Loans applied for.
			a. r. p.	£ s. d.	£ s. d.	£	£
Ulster:							
Antrim,	[illegible]	[illegible]	[illegible]	[illegible]	[illegible]	[illegible]	[illegible]
Armagh,	[illegible]	[illegible]	[illegible]	[illegible]	[illegible]	[illegible]	[illegible]
Cavan,	[illegible]	[illegible]	[illegible]	[illegible]	[illegible]	[illegible]	[illegible]
Donegal,	[illegible]	[illegible]	[illegible]	[illegible]	[illegible]	[illegible]	[illegible]
Down,	[illegible]	[illegible]	[illegible]	[illegible]	[illegible]	[illegible]	[illegible]
Fermanagh,	[illegible]	[illegible]	[illegible]	[illegible]	[illegible]	[illegible]	[illegible]
Londonderry,	[illegible]	[illegible]	[illegible]	[illegible]	[illegible]	[illegible]	[illegible]
Monaghan,	[illegible]	[illegible]	[illegible]	[illegible]	[illegible]	[illegible]	[illegible]
Tyrone,	[illegible]	[illegible]	[illegible]	[illegible]	[illegible]	[illegible]	[illegible]
Total,	[illegible]	[illegible]	[illegible]	[illegible]	[illegible]	[illegible]	[illegible]
Leinster:							
Carlow,	[illegible]	[illegible]	[illegible]	[illegible]	[illegible]	[illegible]	[illegible]
Dublin,	[illegible]	[illegible]	[illegible]	[illegible]	[illegible]	[illegible]	[illegible]
Kildare,	[illegible]	[illegible]	[illegible]	[illegible]	[illegible]	[illegible]	[illegible]
Kilkenny,	[illegible]	[illegible]	[illegible]	[illegible]	[illegible]	[illegible]	[illegible]
King's,	[illegible]	[illegible]	[illegible]	[illegible]	[illegible]	[illegible]	[illegible]
Longford,	[illegible]	[illegible]	[illegible]	[illegible]	[illegible]	[illegible]	[illegible]
Louth,	[illegible]	[illegible]	[illegible]	[illegible]	[illegible]	[illegible]	[illegible]
Meath,	[illegible]	[illegible]	[illegible]	[illegible]	[illegible]	[illegible]	[illegible]
Queen's,	[illegible]	[illegible]	[illegible]	[illegible]	[illegible]	[illegible]	[illegible]
Westmeath,	[illegible]	[illegible]	[illegible]	[illegible]	[illegible]	[illegible]	[illegible]
Wexford,	[illegible]	[illegible]	[illegible]	[illegible]	[illegible]	[illegible]	[illegible]
Wicklow,	[illegible]	[illegible]	[illegible]	[illegible]	[illegible]	[illegible]	[illegible]
Total,	[illegible]	[illegible]	[illegible]	[illegible]	[illegible]	[illegible]	[illegible]
Connaught:							
Galway,	[illegible]	[illegible]	[illegible]	[illegible]	[illegible]	[illegible]	[illegible]
Leitrim,	[illegible]	[illegible]	[illegible]	[illegible]	[illegible]	[illegible]	[illegible]
Mayo,	[illegible]	[illegible]	[illegible]	[illegible]	[illegible]	[illegible]	[illegible]
Roscommon,	[illegible]	[illegible]	[illegible]	[illegible]	[illegible]	[illegible]	[illegible]
Sligo,	[illegible]	[illegible]	[illegible]	[illegible]	[illegible]	[illegible]	[illegible]
Total,	[illegible]	[illegible]	[illegible]	[illegible]	[illegible]	[illegible]	[illegible]
Munster:							
Clare,	[illegible]	[illegible]	[illegible]	[illegible]	[illegible]	[illegible]	[illegible]
Cork,	[illegible]	[illegible]	[illegible]	[illegible]	[illegible]	[illegible]	[illegible]
Kerry,	[illegible]	[illegible]	[illegible]	[illegible]	[illegible]	[illegible]	[illegible]
Limerick,	[illegible]	[illegible]	[illegible]	[illegible]	[illegible]	[illegible]	[illegible]
Tipperary,	[illegible]	[illegible]	[illegible]	[illegible]	[illegible]	[illegible]	[illegible]
Waterford,	[illegible]	[illegible]	[illegible]	[illegible]	[illegible]	[illegible]	[illegible]
Total,	[illegible]	[illegible]	[illegible]	[illegible]	[illegible]	[illegible]	[illegible]
Summary.							
Ulster,	[illegible]	[illegible]	[illegible]	[illegible]	[illegible]	[illegible]	[illegible]
Leinster,	[illegible]	[illegible]	[illegible]	[illegible]	[illegible]	[illegible]	[illegible]
Connaught,	[illegible]	[illegible]	[illegible]	[illegible]	[illegible]	[illegible]	[illegible]
Munster,	[illegible]	[illegible]	[illegible]	[illegible]	[illegible]	[illegible]	[illegible]
Total,	[illegible]	[illegible]	[illegible]	[illegible]	[illegible]	[illegible]	[illegible]

(a) The number of Tenants is the same as the number of Loans.
(b) [illegible]
(c) [illegible]

LIV.—Return showing, according to Provinces and Counties, the Number of Loans provisionally sanctioned, the Rental and Total Purchase-money of the Holdings, and the Amount of Loans sanctioned, also the Number of years' purchase of Rent, during year ended 31st August, 1898.

Provinces and Counties.	No. of Tenants (a)	Rent (b)	Amount of Purchase-money	Amount of Loans	No. of years' purchase of Rent
		£ s. d.	£	£	
Ulster:					
Antrim,	[illegible]	[illegible]	[illegible]	[illegible]	[illegible]
Armagh,	[illegible]	[illegible]	[illegible]	[illegible]	[illegible]
Cavan,	[illegible]	[illegible]	[illegible]	[illegible]	[illegible]
Donegal,	[illegible]	[illegible]	[illegible]	[illegible]	[illegible]
Down,	[illegible]	[illegible]	[illegible]	[illegible]	[illegible]
Fermanagh,	[illegible]	[illegible]	[illegible]	[illegible]	[illegible]
Londonderry,	[illegible]	[illegible]	[illegible]	[illegible]	[illegible]
Monaghan,	[illegible]	[illegible]	[illegible]	[illegible]	[illegible]
Tyrone,	[illegible]	[illegible]	[illegible]	[illegible]	[illegible]
Total,	[illegible]	[illegible]	[illegible]	[illegible]	—
Leinster:					
Carlow,	[illegible]	[illegible]	[illegible]	[illegible]	[illegible]
Dublin,	[illegible]	[illegible]	[illegible]	[illegible]	[illegible]
Kildare,	[illegible]	[illegible]	[illegible]	[illegible]	[illegible]
Kilkenny,	[illegible]	[illegible]	[illegible]	[illegible]	[illegible]
King's,	[illegible]	[illegible]	[illegible]	[illegible]	[illegible]
Longford,	[illegible]	[illegible]	[illegible]	[illegible]	[illegible]
Louth,	[illegible]	[illegible]	[illegible]	[illegible]	[illegible]
Meath,	[illegible]	[illegible]	[illegible]	[illegible]	[illegible]
Queen's,	[illegible]	[illegible]	[illegible]	[illegible]	[illegible]
Westmeath,	[illegible]	[illegible]	[illegible]	[illegible]	[illegible]
Wexford,	[illegible]	[illegible]	[illegible]	[illegible]	[illegible]
Wicklow,	[illegible]	[illegible]	[illegible]	[illegible]	[illegible]
Total,	[illegible]	[illegible]	[illegible]	[illegible]	—
Connaught:					
Galway,	[illegible]	[illegible]	[illegible]	[illegible]	[illegible]
Leitrim,	[illegible]	[illegible]	[illegible]	[illegible]	[illegible]
Mayo,	[illegible]	[illegible]	[illegible]	[illegible]	[illegible]
Roscommon,	[illegible]	[illegible]	[illegible]	[illegible]	[illegible]
Sligo,	[illegible]	[illegible]	[illegible]	[illegible]	[illegible]
Total,	[illegible]	[illegible]	[illegible]	[illegible]	—
Munster:					
Clare,	[illegible]	[illegible]	[illegible]	[illegible]	[illegible]
Cork,	[illegible]	[illegible]	[illegible]	[illegible]	[illegible]
Kerry,	[illegible]	[illegible]	[illegible]	[illegible]	[illegible]
Limerick,	[illegible]	[illegible]	[illegible]	[illegible]	[illegible]
Tipperary,	[illegible]	[illegible]	[illegible]	[illegible]	[illegible]
Waterford,	[illegible]	[illegible]	[illegible]	[illegible]	[illegible]
Total,	[illegible]	[illegible]	[illegible]	[illegible]	—
SUMMARY					
Ulster,	[illegible]	[illegible]	[illegible]	[illegible]	[illegible]
Leinster,	[illegible]	[illegible]	[illegible]	[illegible]	[illegible]
Connaught,	[illegible]	[illegible]	[illegible]	[illegible]	[illegible]
Munster,	[illegible]	[illegible]	[illegible]	[illegible]	[illegible]
Total,	[illegible]	[illegible]	[illegible]	[illegible]	[illegible]

(a) The Number of Tenants is the same as the number of Loans.

(b) The Rents stated in this Return are the Rents payable by the Tenants previous to the sale, except in a few cases [illegible]

IV.—Return showing, according to Provinces and Counties, the Number of Loans provisionally sanctioned, the Rental and Total Purchase-money of the Holdings, and the Amount of Loans sanctioned, also the Number of Years' Purchase of Rent, during Five Years ended 21st August, 1890.

Province and County.	No. of Loans (a).	Rental (b).	Amount of Purchase-money.	Amount of Loans.	No. of years' purchase of Rent.
Ulster:		£ s. d.	£	£	
Antrim,	[illegible]	[illegible]	[illegible]	[illegible]	[illegible]
Armagh,	[illegible]	[illegible]	[illegible]	[illegible]	[illegible]
Cavan,	[illegible]	[illegible]	[illegible]	[illegible]	[illegible]
Donegal,	[illegible]	[illegible]	[illegible]	[illegible]	[illegible]
Down,	[illegible]	[illegible]	[illegible]	[illegible]	[illegible]
Fermanagh,	[illegible]	[illegible]	[illegible]	[illegible]	[illegible]
Londonderry,	[illegible]	[illegible]	[illegible]	[illegible]	[illegible]
Monaghan,	[illegible]	[illegible]	[illegible]	[illegible]	[illegible]
Tyrone,	[illegible]	[illegible]	[illegible]	[illegible]	[illegible]
Total,	[illegible]	[illegible]	[illegible]	[illegible]	—
Leinster:					
Carlow,	[illegible]	[illegible]	[illegible]	[illegible]	[illegible]
Dublin,	[illegible]	[illegible]	[illegible]	[illegible]	[illegible]
Kildare,	[illegible]	[illegible]	[illegible]	[illegible]	[illegible]
Kilkenny,	[illegible]	[illegible]	[illegible]	[illegible]	[illegible]
King's,	[illegible]	[illegible]	[illegible]	[illegible]	[illegible]
Longford,	[illegible]	[illegible]	[illegible]	[illegible]	[illegible]
Louth,	[illegible]	[illegible]	[illegible]	[illegible]	[illegible]
Meath,	[illegible]	[illegible]	[illegible]	[illegible]	[illegible]
Queen's,	[illegible]	[illegible]	[illegible]	[illegible]	[illegible]
Westmeath,	[illegible]	[illegible]	[illegible]	[illegible]	[illegible]
Wexford,	[illegible]	[illegible]	[illegible]	[illegible]	[illegible]
Wicklow,	[illegible]	[illegible]	[illegible]	[illegible]	[illegible]
Total,	[illegible]	[illegible]	[illegible]	[illegible]	—
Connaught:					
Galway,	[illegible]	[illegible]	[illegible]	[illegible]	[illegible]
Leitrim,	[illegible]	[illegible]	[illegible]	[illegible]	[illegible]
Mayo,	[illegible]	[illegible]	[illegible]	[illegible]	[illegible]
Roscommon,	[illegible]	[illegible]	[illegible]	[illegible]	[illegible]
Sligo,	[illegible]	[illegible]	[illegible]	[illegible]	[illegible]
Total,	[illegible]	[illegible]	[illegible]	[illegible]	—
Munster:					
Clare,	[illegible]	[illegible]	[illegible]	[illegible]	[illegible]
Cork,	[illegible]	[illegible]	[illegible]	[illegible]	[illegible]
Kerry,	[illegible]	[illegible]	[illegible]	[illegible]	[illegible]
Limerick,	[illegible]	[illegible]	[illegible]	[illegible]	[illegible]
Tipperary,	[illegible]	[illegible]	[illegible]	[illegible]	[illegible]
Waterford,	[illegible]	[illegible]	[illegible]	[illegible]	[illegible]
Total,	[illegible]	[illegible]	[illegible]	[illegible]	—
SUMMARY.					
Ulster,	[illegible]	[illegible]	[illegible]	[illegible]	[illegible]
Leinster,	[illegible]	[illegible]	[illegible]	[illegible]	[illegible]
Connaught,	[illegible]	[illegible]	[illegible]	[illegible]	[illegible]
Munster,	[illegible]	[illegible]	[illegible]	[illegible]	[illegible]
Total,	[illegible]	[illegible]	[illegible]	[illegible]	[illegible]

(a) The number of Tenants is the same as the number of Loans.

(b) The Rental is the ... Rent, or the Rent payable by the Tenants ... [illegible] ... payable by the Tenants.

LVI.—Return showing, according to Provinces and Counties, the Number of Loans issued, the Number of Estates, and the Total Acreage, Tenement Valuation, and Rental of the Holdings in respect of which the Loans have been issued, also the Total Purchase-money and the Amount of Loans obtained from Land Commission, and the Number of Years' purchase of Rent, during Year ended 31st August, 189[illegible].

Provinces and Counties.	No. of Loans. (a)	No. of Estates.	Acreage in Statute Measure.	Tenement Valuation. (b)	Rent. (c)	Purchase-money agreed upon.	Amount of Loans.	No. of years' Purchase of Rent.
			A. R. P.	£ s. d.	£ s. d.	£	£	
Ulster:								
Antrim,	[illegible]	[illegible]	[illegible]	[illegible]	[illegible]	[illegible]	[illegible]	[illegible]
Armagh,	[illegible]	[illegible]	[illegible]	[illegible]	[illegible]	[illegible]	[illegible]	[illegible]
Cavan,	[illegible]	[illegible]	[illegible]	[illegible]	[illegible]	[illegible]	[illegible]	[illegible]
Donegal,	[illegible]	[illegible]	[illegible]	[illegible]	[illegible]	[illegible]	[illegible]	[illegible]
Down,	[illegible]	[illegible]	[illegible]	[illegible]	[illegible]	[illegible]	[illegible]	[illegible]
Fermanagh,	[illegible]	[illegible]	[illegible]	[illegible]	[illegible]	[illegible]	[illegible]	[illegible]
Londonderry,	[illegible]	[illegible]	[illegible]	[illegible]	[illegible]	[illegible]	[illegible]	[illegible]
Monaghan,	[illegible]	[illegible]	[illegible]	[illegible]	[illegible]	[illegible]	[illegible]	[illegible]
Tyrone,	[illegible]	[illegible]	[illegible]	[illegible]	[illegible]	[illegible]	[illegible]	[illegible]
Total,	[illegible]	[illegible]	[illegible]	[illegible]	[illegible]	[illegible]	[illegible]	—
Leinster:								
Carlow,	[illegible]	[illegible]	[illegible]	[illegible]	[illegible]	[illegible]	[illegible]	[illegible]
Dublin,	[illegible]	[illegible]	[illegible]	[illegible]	[illegible]	[illegible]	[illegible]	[illegible]
Kildare,	[illegible]	[illegible]	[illegible]	[illegible]	[illegible]	[illegible]	[illegible]	[illegible]
Kilkenny,	[illegible]	[illegible]	[illegible]	[illegible]	[illegible]	[illegible]	[illegible]	[illegible]
King's,	[illegible]	[illegible]	[illegible]	[illegible]	[illegible]	[illegible]	[illegible]	[illegible]
Longford,	[illegible]	[illegible]	[illegible]	[illegible]	[illegible]	[illegible]	[illegible]	[illegible]
Louth,	[illegible]	[illegible]	[illegible]	[illegible]	[illegible]	[illegible]	[illegible]	[illegible]
Meath,	[illegible]	[illegible]	[illegible]	[illegible]	[illegible]	[illegible]	[illegible]	[illegible]
Queen's,	[illegible]	[illegible]	[illegible]	[illegible]	[illegible]	[illegible]	[illegible]	[illegible]
Westmeath,	[illegible]	[illegible]	[illegible]	[illegible]	[illegible]	[illegible]	[illegible]	[illegible]
Wexford,	[illegible]	[illegible]	[illegible]	[illegible]	[illegible]	[illegible]	[illegible]	[illegible]
Wicklow,	[illegible]	[illegible]	[illegible]	[illegible]	[illegible]	[illegible]	[illegible]	[illegible]
Total,	[illegible]	[illegible]	[illegible]	[illegible]	[illegible]	[illegible]	[illegible]	—
Connaught:								
Galway,	[illegible]	[illegible]	[illegible]	[illegible]	[illegible]	[illegible]	[illegible]	[illegible]
Leitrim,	[illegible]	[illegible]	[illegible]	[illegible]	[illegible]	[illegible]	[illegible]	[illegible]
Mayo,	[illegible]	[illegible]	[illegible]	[illegible]	[illegible]	[illegible]	[illegible]	[illegible]
Roscommon,	[illegible]	[illegible]	[illegible]	[illegible]	[illegible]	[illegible]	[illegible]	[illegible]
Sligo,	[illegible]	[illegible]	[illegible]	[illegible]	[illegible]	[illegible]	[illegible]	[illegible]
Total,	[illegible]	[illegible]	[illegible]	[illegible]	[illegible]	[illegible]	[illegible]	—
Munster:								
Clare,	[illegible]	[illegible]	[illegible]	[illegible]	[illegible]	[illegible]	[illegible]	[illegible]
Cork,	[illegible]	[illegible]	[illegible]	[illegible]	[illegible]	[illegible]	[illegible]	[illegible]
Kerry,	[illegible]	[illegible]	[illegible]	[illegible]	[illegible]	[illegible]	[illegible]	[illegible]
Limerick,	[illegible]	[illegible]	[illegible]	[illegible]	[illegible]	[illegible]	[illegible]	[illegible]
Tipperary,	[illegible]	[illegible]	[illegible]	[illegible]	[illegible]	[illegible]	[illegible]	[illegible]
Waterford,	[illegible]	[illegible]	[illegible]	[illegible]	[illegible]	[illegible]	[illegible]	[illegible]
Total,	[illegible]	[illegible]	[illegible]	[illegible]	[illegible]	[illegible]	[illegible]	—
SUMMARY.								
Ulster,	[illegible]	[illegible]	[illegible]	[illegible]	[illegible]	[illegible]	[illegible]	[illegible]
Leinster,	[illegible]	[illegible]	[illegible]	[illegible]	[illegible]	[illegible]	[illegible]	[illegible]
Connaught,	[illegible]	[illegible]	[illegible]	[illegible]	[illegible]	[illegible]	[illegible]	[illegible]
Munster,	[illegible]	[illegible]	[illegible]	[illegible]	[illegible]	[illegible]	[illegible]	[illegible]
Total,	[illegible]	[illegible]	[illegible]	[illegible]	[illegible]	[illegible]	[illegible]	[illegible]

(a) The number of Tenants is the same as the number of Loans.

(b) [illegible]

(c) [illegible]

LVII.—Return showing, according to Provinces and Counties, the number of Loans issued, the number of Estates, and the Total Acreage, Tenement Valuation, and Rental of the Holdings in respect of which Loans have been issued, also the Total Purchase-money and the Amount of Loans obtained from Land Commission, and the Number of Years' purchase of Rent, during the years ended 31st August, 1890.

Province and County	No. of Loans (a)	No. of Estates	Acreage in Statute Measure	Tenement Valuation (b)	Rent (c)	Purchase-money agreed upon	Amount of Loans	No. of years' purchase of Rent
			A. R. P.	£ s. d.	£ s. d.	£	£	
Ulster:								
Antrim,	[illegible]	[illegible]	[illegible]	[illegible]	[illegible]	[illegible]	[illegible]	[illegible]
Armagh,	[illegible]	[illegible]	[illegible]	[illegible]	[illegible]	[illegible]	[illegible]	[illegible]
Cavan,	[illegible]	[illegible]	[illegible]	[illegible]	[illegible]	[illegible]	[illegible]	[illegible]
Donegal,	[illegible]	[illegible]	[illegible]	[illegible]	[illegible]	[illegible]	[illegible]	[illegible]
Down,	[illegible]	[illegible]	[illegible]	[illegible]	[illegible]	[illegible]	[illegible]	[illegible]
Fermanagh,	[illegible]	[illegible]	[illegible]	[illegible]	[illegible]	[illegible]	[illegible]	[illegible]
Londonderry,	[illegible]	[illegible]	[illegible]	[illegible]	[illegible]	[illegible]	[illegible]	[illegible]
Monaghan,	[illegible]	[illegible]	[illegible]	[illegible]	[illegible]	[illegible]	[illegible]	[illegible]
Tyrone,	[illegible]	[illegible]	[illegible]	[illegible]	[illegible]	[illegible]	[illegible]	[illegible]
Total,	[illegible]	[illegible]	[illegible]	[illegible]	[illegible]	[illegible]	[illegible]	—
Leinster:								
Carlow,	[illegible]	[illegible]	[illegible]	[illegible]	[illegible]	[illegible]	[illegible]	[illegible]
Dublin,	[illegible]	[illegible]	[illegible]	[illegible]	[illegible]	[illegible]	[illegible]	[illegible]
Kildare,	[illegible]	[illegible]	[illegible]	[illegible]	[illegible]	[illegible]	[illegible]	[illegible]
Kilkenny,	[illegible]	[illegible]	[illegible]	[illegible]	[illegible]	[illegible]	[illegible]	[illegible]
King's,	[illegible]	[illegible]	[illegible]	[illegible]	[illegible]	[illegible]	[illegible]	[illegible]
Longford,	[illegible]	[illegible]	[illegible]	[illegible]	[illegible]	[illegible]	[illegible]	[illegible]
Louth,	[illegible]	[illegible]	[illegible]	[illegible]	[illegible]	[illegible]	[illegible]	[illegible]
Meath,	[illegible]	[illegible]	[illegible]	[illegible]	[illegible]	[illegible]	[illegible]	[illegible]
Queen's,	[illegible]	[illegible]	[illegible]	[illegible]	[illegible]	[illegible]	[illegible]	[illegible]
Westmeath,	[illegible]	[illegible]	[illegible]	[illegible]	[illegible]	[illegible]	[illegible]	[illegible]
Wexford,	[illegible]	[illegible]	[illegible]	[illegible]	[illegible]	[illegible]	[illegible]	[illegible]
Wicklow,	[illegible]	[illegible]	[illegible]	[illegible]	[illegible]	[illegible]	[illegible]	[illegible]
Total,	[illegible]	[illegible]	[illegible]	[illegible]	[illegible]	[illegible]	[illegible]	—
Connaught:								
Galway,	[illegible]	[illegible]	[illegible]	[illegible]	[illegible]	[illegible]	[illegible]	[illegible]
Leitrim,	[illegible]	[illegible]	[illegible]	[illegible]	[illegible]	[illegible]	[illegible]	[illegible]
Mayo,	[illegible]	[illegible]	[illegible]	[illegible]	[illegible]	[illegible]	[illegible]	[illegible]
Roscommon,	[illegible]	[illegible]	[illegible]	[illegible]	[illegible]	[illegible]	[illegible]	[illegible]
Sligo,	[illegible]	[illegible]	[illegible]	[illegible]	[illegible]	[illegible]	[illegible]	[illegible]
Total,	[illegible]	[illegible]	[illegible]	[illegible]	[illegible]	[illegible]	[illegible]	—
Munster:								
Clare,	[illegible]	[illegible]	[illegible]	[illegible]	[illegible]	[illegible]	[illegible]	[illegible]
Cork,	[illegible]	[illegible]	[illegible]	[illegible]	[illegible]	[illegible]	[illegible]	[illegible]
Kerry,	[illegible]	[illegible]	[illegible]	[illegible]	[illegible]	[illegible]	[illegible]	[illegible]
Limerick,	[illegible]	[illegible]	[illegible]	[illegible]	[illegible]	[illegible]	[illegible]	[illegible]
Tipperary,	[illegible]	[illegible]	[illegible]	[illegible]	[illegible]	[illegible]	[illegible]	[illegible]
Waterford,	[illegible]	[illegible]	[illegible]	[illegible]	[illegible]	[illegible]	[illegible]	[illegible]
Total,	[illegible]	[illegible]	[illegible]	[illegible]	[illegible]	[illegible]	[illegible]	—
SUMMARY.								
Ulster,	[illegible]	[illegible]	[illegible]	[illegible]	[illegible]	[illegible]	[illegible]	[illegible]
Leinster,	[illegible]	[illegible]	[illegible]	[illegible]	[illegible]	[illegible]	[illegible]	[illegible]
Connaught,	[illegible]	[illegible]	[illegible]	[illegible]	[illegible]	[illegible]	[illegible]	[illegible]
Munster,	[illegible]	[illegible]	[illegible]	[illegible]	[illegible]	[illegible]	[illegible]	[illegible]
Total,	[illegible]	[illegible]	[illegible]	[illegible]	[illegible]	[illegible]	[illegible]	[illegible]

LVIII.—RETURN showing, according to Provinces and Counties, the Number of Estates purchased by the Irish Land Commission under section 6, with the Number of Tenants, the Acreage, Tenement Valuation, Rental, Purchase Money, and amount of Loans, during Year ended 21st August, 1890.

Province and County.	Number of Estates.	Number of Tenants.	Acreage in Statute Measure.	Tenement Valuation. (b)	Rental.	Purchase Money.	Amount of Loans.
			A. R. P.	£ s. d.	£ s. d.	£	£
ULSTER.							
Cavan,	[illegible]	[illegible]	[illegible]	[illegible]	[illegible]	[illegible]	[illegible]
Tyrone,	[illegible]	[illegible]	[illegible]	[illegible]	[illegible]	[illegible]	[illegible]
Total,	[illegible]	[illegible]	[illegible]	[illegible]	[illegible]	[illegible]	[illegible]
LEINSTER.							
Kilkenny,	[illegible]	[illegible]	[illegible]	[illegible]	[illegible]	[illegible]	[illegible]
Total,	[illegible]	[illegible]	[illegible]	[illegible]	[illegible]	[illegible]	[illegible]
CONNAUGHT.							
Galway,	[illegible]	[illegible]	[illegible]	[illegible]	[illegible]	[illegible]	[illegible]
Leitrim,	[illegible]	[illegible]	[illegible]	[illegible]	[illegible]	[illegible]	[illegible]
Total,	[illegible]	[illegible]	[illegible]	[illegible]	[illegible]	[illegible]	[illegible]
MUNSTER.							
Clare,	[illegible]	[illegible]	[illegible]	[illegible]	[illegible]	[illegible]	[illegible]
Cork,	[illegible]	[illegible]	[illegible]	[illegible]	[illegible]	[illegible]	[illegible]
Tipperary,	[illegible]	[illegible]	[illegible]	[illegible]	[illegible]	[illegible]	[illegible]
Total,	[illegible]	[illegible]	[illegible]	[illegible]	[illegible]	[illegible]	[illegible]
SUMMARY.							
Ulster,	[illegible]	[illegible]	[illegible]	[illegible]	[illegible]	[illegible]	[illegible]
Leinster,	[illegible]	[illegible]	[illegible]	[illegible]	[illegible]	[illegible]	[illegible]
Connaught,	[illegible]	[illegible]	[illegible]	[illegible]	[illegible]	[illegible]	[illegible]
Munster,	[illegible]	[illegible]	[illegible]	[illegible]	[illegible]	[illegible]	[illegible]
Total,	[illegible]	[illegible]	[illegible]	[illegible]	[illegible]	[illegible]	[illegible]

NOTE.—Particulars of above Estates are included in Returns LIV. to LVII., inclusive.

(a) [illegible]

(b) [illegible]

LIX.—RETURN showing, according to Provinces and Counties, the number of Estates purchased by the Irish Land Commission under Section 6, with the Number of Tenants, the Acreage, Tenement Valuation, Rental, Purchase Money, and Amount of Loans, during Five Years ended 31st August, 1890.

Province and County.	No. of Estates.	No. of Tenants.	Acreage.	Tenement Valuation. (a)	Rental.	Purchase Money.	Amount of Loans.
			A. R. P.	£ s. d.	£ s. d.	£	£
ULSTER:							
Antrim,	[illegible]	[illegible]	[illegible]	611 16 6	[illegible]	[illegible]	[illegible]
Armagh,	[illegible]	[illegible]	[illegible]	[illegible]	[illegible]	[illegible]	[illegible]
Cavan,	[illegible]	[illegible]	[illegible]	[illegible]	[illegible]	[illegible]	[illegible]
Donegal,	[illegible]	[illegible]	[illegible]	[illegible]	[illegible]	[illegible]	[illegible]
Tyrone,	[illegible]	[illegible]	[illegible]	[illegible]	[illegible]	[illegible]	[illegible]
Total,	[illegible]	[illegible]	[illegible]	[illegible]	[illegible]	[illegible]	[illegible]
LEINSTER:							
Dublin,	[illegible]	[illegible]	[illegible]	[illegible]	[illegible]	[illegible]	[illegible]
Kilkenny,	[illegible]	[illegible]	[illegible]	[illegible]	[illegible]	[illegible]	[illegible]
Meath,	[illegible]	[illegible]	[illegible]	[illegible]	[illegible]	[illegible]	[illegible]
Queen's,	[illegible]	[illegible]	[illegible]	[illegible]	[illegible]	[illegible]	[illegible]
Wexford,	[illegible]	[illegible]	[illegible]	[illegible]	[illegible]	[illegible]	[illegible]
Total,	[illegible]	[illegible]	[illegible]	[illegible]	[illegible]	[illegible]	[illegible]
CONNAUGHT:							
Galway,	[illegible]	[illegible]	[illegible]	[illegible]	[illegible]	[illegible]	[illegible]
Leitrim,	[illegible]	[illegible]	[illegible]	[illegible]	[illegible]	[illegible]	[illegible]
Mayo,	[illegible]	[illegible]	[illegible]	[illegible]	[illegible]	[illegible]	[illegible]
Roscommon,	[illegible]	[illegible]	[illegible]	[illegible]	[illegible]	[illegible]	[illegible]
Total,	[illegible]	[illegible]	[illegible]	[illegible]	[illegible]	[illegible]	[illegible]
MUNSTER:							
Clare,	[illegible]	[illegible]	[illegible]	[illegible]	[illegible]	[illegible]	[illegible]
Cork,	[illegible]	[illegible]	[illegible]	[illegible]	[illegible]	[illegible]	[illegible]
Tipperary,	[illegible]	[illegible]	[illegible]	[illegible]	[illegible]	[illegible]	[illegible]
Waterford,	[illegible]	[illegible]	[illegible]	[illegible]	[illegible]	[illegible]	[illegible]
Total,	[illegible]	[illegible]	[illegible]	[illegible]	[illegible]	[illegible]	[illegible]
SUMMARY:							
Ulster,	[illegible]	[illegible]	[illegible]	[illegible]	[illegible]	[illegible]	[illegible]
Leinster,	[illegible]	[illegible]	[illegible]	[illegible]	[illegible]	[illegible]	[illegible]
Connaught,	[illegible]	[illegible]	[illegible]	[illegible]	[illegible]	[illegible]	[illegible]
Munster,	[illegible]	[illegible]	[illegible]	[illegible]	[illegible]	[illegible]	[illegible]
Total,	[illegible]	[illegible]	[illegible]	[illegible]	[illegible]	[illegible]	[illegible]

NOTE.—[illegible] included in Returns LIII. to LVII. [illegible]

(a) [illegible]

Court of the Land Commission in Dublin.

LX.—Table showing the Number of Motions and Applications disposed of in Court under the Land Law (Ireland) Acts, 1881 and 1887, and the Arrears of Rent (Ireland) Act, 1882, during the year ended 21st August, 1890, exclusive of Orders made upon rehearings.

Land Law Acts—

Motions disposed of by Final Orders,	379
Motions ex parte disposed of by Interlocutory Orders and directions,	1,349
Motions on Notice disposed of by Interlocutory Orders and directions,	419
Total,	2,247
Arrears of Rent Act— Motions disposed of by Interlocutory and Final Orders and directions,	0
Total under above Acts,	2,247
Side Bar Orders by Registrar during same period,	8,777

LXI.—Table showing the Number of Motions and Applications disposed of by the Court in Chamber under the Land Law (Ireland) Acts, 1881 and 1887, and the Labourers (Ireland) Acts, 1883 to 1886, during the year ended 21st August, 1890:—

Land Law Acts—

Rents fixed in Leasehold cases—where parties consent,	681
Do. in case of Yearly Tenancies,	64
Labourers Acts— Motions disposed of by Interlocutory and Final Orders and directions,	[illegible]
	3,747

LXII.—Table showing the proceedings under the Labourers (Ireland) Acts, 1883 to 1886, during the year ended 21st August, 1890.

Poor Law Union.	County.	No. of applications received.	Whether disposed of: Disposed.	Whether disposed of: While during.	Cottages.	Average Annual Rent payable as Orders by the Sanitary Authority in respect of such Orders applied.	Compensation other than Rent awarded by Court.
[illegible]	[illegible]	[illegible]	[illegible]	[illegible]	[illegible]	£ s. d. [illegible]	£ s. d.
[illegible]	[illegible]	[illegible]	[illegible]	[illegible]	[illegible]	[illegible]	—
Athy,	[illegible]	[illegible]	[illegible]	[illegible]	3	[illegible]	—
[illegible]	[illegible]	[illegible]	[illegible]	[illegible]	[illegible]	[illegible]	—
[illegible]	[illegible]	[illegible]	[illegible]	[illegible]	[illegible]	[illegible]	—
[illegible]	[illegible]	[illegible]	[illegible]	[illegible]	[illegible]	[illegible]	—
[illegible]	[illegible]	[illegible]	[illegible]	[illegible]	[illegible]	[illegible]	—
Callan,	[illegible]	[illegible]	[illegible]	[illegible]	[illegible]	[illegible]	—
Carlow,	[illegible]	[illegible]	[illegible]	[illegible]	[illegible]	[illegible]	—
[illegible]	[illegible]	[illegible]	[illegible]	[illegible]	[illegible]	[illegible]	—
Celbridge,	[illegible]	[illegible]	[illegible]	[illegible]	[illegible]	[illegible]	[illegible]
[illegible]	[illegible]	[illegible]	[illegible]	[illegible]	[illegible]	[illegible]	—
[illegible]	[illegible]	[illegible]	[illegible]	[illegible]	[illegible]	[illegible]	—
[illegible]	[illegible]	[illegible]	[illegible]	[illegible]	[illegible]	[illegible]	—
[illegible]	[illegible]	[illegible]	[illegible]	[illegible]	[illegible]	[illegible]	—
[illegible]	[illegible]	[illegible]	[illegible]	[illegible]	[illegible]	[illegible]	—
[illegible]	[illegible]	[illegible]	[illegible]	[illegible]	[illegible]	[illegible]	—
[illegible]	[illegible]	[illegible]	[illegible]	[illegible]	[illegible]	[illegible]	—
[illegible]	[illegible]	[illegible]	[illegible]	[illegible]	[illegible]	[illegible]	[illegible]
[illegible]	[illegible]	[illegible]	[illegible]	[illegible]	[illegible]	[illegible]	—
[illegible]	[illegible]	[illegible]	[illegible]	[illegible]	[illegible]	[illegible]	—
[illegible]	[illegible]	[illegible]	[illegible]	[illegible]	[illegible]	[illegible]	—
[illegible]	[illegible]	[illegible]	[illegible]	[illegible]	[illegible]	[illegible]	—
[illegible]	[illegible]	[illegible]	[illegible]	[illegible]	[illegible]	[illegible]	—
[illegible]	[illegible]	[illegible]	[illegible]	[illegible]	[illegible]	[illegible]	—
[illegible]	[illegible]	[illegible]	[illegible]	[illegible]	[illegible]	[illegible]	—
Naas,	[illegible]	[illegible]	[illegible]	[illegible]	[illegible]	[illegible]	—
[illegible]	[illegible]	[illegible]	[illegible]	[illegible]	[illegible]	[illegible]	—
[illegible]	[illegible]	[illegible]	[illegible]	[illegible]	[illegible]	[illegible]	—
[illegible]	[illegible]	[illegible]	[illegible]	[illegible]	[illegible]	[illegible]	—
[illegible]	[illegible]	[illegible]	[illegible]	[illegible]	[illegible]	[illegible]	—
[illegible]	[illegible]	[illegible]	[illegible]	[illegible]	[illegible]	[illegible]	—
[illegible]	[illegible]	[illegible]	[illegible]	[illegible]	[illegible]	[illegible]	—
[illegible]	[illegible]	[illegible]	[illegible]	[illegible]	[illegible]	[illegible]	—
[illegible]	[illegible]	[illegible]	[illegible]	[illegible]	[illegible]	[illegible]	—
[illegible]	[illegible]	[illegible]	[illegible]	[illegible]	[illegible]	[illegible]	—

LXIII.—TABLE showing the Proceedings under the Labourers (Ireland) Acts, 1883 to 1886, during the period ended 31st August, 1890.

Poor Law Union.	County.	No. of Applications lodged.	Number disposed of. Dismissed.	Number disposed of. Withdrawn.	Undecided.	Average Annual Rent payable to Owner by the Sanitary Authority in respect of each Cottage applied under.	Compensation other than Rent awarded by Court.
						£ s. d.	£ s. d.
Abbeyleix	Queen's	[illegible]	[illegible]	[illegible]	[illegible]	[illegible]	[illegible]
Ardee	Louth, Meath	[illegible]	[illegible]	[illegible]	[illegible]	[illegible]	[illegible]
Athy	Kildare, Queen's	[illegible]	[illegible]	[illegible]	[illegible]	[illegible]	[illegible]
[illegible]	Cavan	[illegible]	[illegible]	[illegible]	[illegible]	[illegible]	[illegible]
[illegible]	[illegible]	[illegible]	[illegible]	[illegible]	[illegible]	[illegible]	[illegible]
[illegible]	[illegible]	[illegible]	[illegible]	[illegible]	[illegible]	[illegible]	—
[illegible]	[illegible]	[illegible]	[illegible]	[illegible]	[illegible]	[illegible]	[illegible]
[illegible]	[illegible]	[illegible]	[illegible]	[illegible]	[illegible]	[illegible]	[illegible]
[illegible]	[illegible]	[illegible]	[illegible]	[illegible]	[illegible]	[illegible]	—
Carrick-on-Shannon	[illegible]	[illegible]	[illegible]	[illegible]	[illegible]	[illegible]	[illegible]
[illegible]	[illegible]	[illegible]	[illegible]	[illegible]	[illegible]	[illegible]	[illegible]
[illegible]	[illegible]	[illegible]	[illegible]	[illegible]	[illegible]	[illegible]	[illegible]
[illegible]	[illegible]	[illegible]	[illegible]	[illegible]	[illegible]	—	—
[illegible]	[illegible]	[illegible]	[illegible]	[illegible]	[illegible]	[illegible]	—
[illegible]	[illegible]	[illegible]	[illegible]	[illegible]	[illegible]	[illegible]	—
[illegible]	[illegible]	[illegible]	[illegible]	[illegible]	[illegible]	[illegible]	[illegible]
[illegible]	[illegible]	[illegible]	[illegible]	[illegible]	[illegible]	—	—
[illegible]	[illegible]	[illegible]	[illegible]	[illegible]	[illegible]	[illegible]	[illegible]
[illegible]	[illegible]	[illegible]	[illegible]	[illegible]	[illegible]	[illegible]	—
[illegible]	[illegible]	[illegible]	[illegible]	[illegible]	[illegible]	[illegible]	—
[illegible]	[illegible]	[illegible]	[illegible]	[illegible]	[illegible]	[illegible]	[illegible]
[illegible]	[illegible]	[illegible]	[illegible]	[illegible]	[illegible]	[illegible]	[illegible]
[illegible]	[illegible]	[illegible]	[illegible]	[illegible]	[illegible]	[illegible]	[illegible]
[illegible]	[illegible]	[illegible]	[illegible]	[illegible]	[illegible]	[illegible]	—
[illegible]	[illegible]	[illegible]	[illegible]	[illegible]	[illegible]	[illegible]	—
[illegible]	[illegible]	[illegible]	[illegible]	[illegible]	[illegible]	—	—
[illegible]	[illegible]	[illegible]	[illegible]	[illegible]	[illegible]	[illegible]	—
[illegible]	[illegible]	[illegible]	[illegible]	[illegible]	[illegible]	[illegible]	[illegible]
[illegible]	[illegible]	[illegible]	[illegible]	[illegible]	[illegible]	[illegible]	[illegible]
[illegible]	[illegible]	[illegible]	[illegible]	[illegible]	[illegible]	[illegible]	—
[illegible]	[illegible]	[illegible]	[illegible]	[illegible]	[illegible]	[illegible]	[illegible]
[illegible]	[illegible]	[illegible]	[illegible]	[illegible]	[illegible]	[illegible]	[illegible]
[illegible]	[illegible]	[illegible]	[illegible]	[illegible]	[illegible]	[illegible]	[illegible]
[illegible]	[illegible]	[illegible]	[illegible]	[illegible]	[illegible]	[illegible]	[illegible]
[illegible]	[illegible]	[illegible]	[illegible]	[illegible]	[illegible]	[illegible]	—
[illegible]	[illegible]	[illegible]	[illegible]	[illegible]	[illegible]	[illegible]	[illegible]
[illegible]	[illegible]	[illegible]	[illegible]	[illegible]	[illegible]	[illegible]	[illegible]
[illegible]	[illegible]	[illegible]	[illegible]	[illegible]	[illegible]	[illegible]	—
[illegible]	[illegible]	[illegible]	[illegible]	[illegible]	[illegible]	[illegible]	—
[illegible]	[illegible]	[illegible]	[illegible]	[illegible]	[illegible]	[illegible]	[illegible]

Applications to set aside Leases or Grants.

Land Law (Ireland) Act, 1887, Sec. 2.

Tables LXIV. to LXVII., inclusive.

LXIV.—Table showing the Number of Applications by Lessee or Grantee to the Land Commission to have Lease or Grant executed since 1st January, 1869, declared void (Form 80), during the Year ended 21st August, 1890.

Provinces and Counties.	Number of applications lodged.	Declared void.	Dismissed or struck out.	Withdrawn.	Number of applications pending.
Ulster:					
Antrim,	–	–	[illegible]	–	[illegible]
Donegal,	–	–	[illegible]	–	–
Down,	–	–	[illegible]	–	[illegible]
Fermanagh,	–	–	[illegible]	–	–
Total of Ulster,	–	–	[illegible]	–	[illegible]
Leinster:					
Dublin,	–	–	–	–	[illegible]
Westmeath,	–	–	[illegible]	–	–
Total of Leinster,	–	–	[illegible]	–	[illegible]
Connaught:					
Galway,	–	–	–	–	[illegible]
Mayo,	–	–	[illegible]	–	–
Total of Connaught,	–	–	[illegible]	–	[illegible]
Munster:					
Clare,	–	–	–	–	[illegible]
Tipperary,	–	–	–	–	[illegible]
Total of Munster,	–	–	–	–	[illegible]
Total of Ireland,	–	–	[illegible]	–	[illegible]

LXV.—Table showing the Number of Applications by Lessee or Grantee to the Land Commission to have Lease or Grant executed since 1st January, 1869, declared void (Form 80), during the three years ended 21st August, 1890.

LXVI.—Table showing the Number of Applications by Lessee or Grantee to the Civil Bill Courts to have Lease or Grant executed since 1st January, 1889, declared void (Form 50) during the year ended 31st August, 1890.

Provinces and Counties.	Number of applications received.	Declared void.	Dismissed or struck out.	Withdrawn.	Number of applications pending.
Ulster.					
Antrim,	[illegible]	[illegible]	[illegible]	[illegible]	[illegible]
Total of Ireland,	[illegible]	[illegible]	[illegible]	[illegible]	[illegible]

LXVII.—Table showing the Number of Applications by Lessee or Grantee to the Civil Bill Courts to have Lease or Grant executed since 1st January, 1880, declared void (Form 60) during the three years ended 31st August, 1890.

Provinces and Counties.	Number of applications received.	Declared void.	Dismissed or struck out.	Withdrawn.	Number of applications pending.
Ulster:					
Antrim,	[illegible]	–	–	–	[illegible]
Londonderry,	1	–	1	–	–
Total of Ulster,	4	–	1	–	[illegible]
Connaught:					
Mayo,	5	–	[illegible]	–	
Total of Connaught,	[illegible]	–	[illegible]	–	–
Total of Ireland,	[illegible]	–	[illegible]	–	[illegible]

Leaseholders declared Present Tenants.

Land Law (Ireland) Act, 1887, *Sec.* 1.

Tables LXVIII. to LXXI., inclusive.

LXVIII.—Table showing the Number of Applications by Leaseholders to the Land Commission to be declared Tenants of present tenancies (Form 81) during the year ended 21st August, [illegible].

Province and County.	Number of applications received.	Declared present Tenants.	Dismissed or struck out.	Withdrawn.	Number of applications pending.
Ulster:					
Antrim,	[illegible]	[illegible]	-	-	[illegible]
Armagh,	-	-	-	-	-
Cavan,	[illegible]	75	-	-	-
Donegal,	-	-	-	[illegible]	
Down,	[illegible]	[illegible]	-	-	-
Fermanagh,	-	-	-	-	[illegible]
Londonderry,	[illegible]	[illegible]	[illegible]	[illegible]	[illegible]
Monaghan,	-	-	-	-	-
Tyrone,	[illegible]	[illegible]	-	-	[illegible]
Total of Ulster,	[illegible]	[illegible]	[illegible]	[illegible]	[illegible]
Leinster:					
Carlow,	[illegible]	[illegible]	[illegible]	-	[illegible]
Dublin,	[illegible]	[illegible]	[illegible]	[illegible]	-
Kildare,	-	[illegible]	-	-	-
Kilkenny,	[illegible]	[illegible]	-	-	[illegible]
King's,	-	[illegible]	-	-	-
Longford,	[illegible]	-	-	-	[illegible]
Louth,	-	-	-	-	-
Meath,	[illegible]	[illegible]	-	-	[illegible]
Queen's,	[illegible]	-	-	-	[illegible]
Westmeath,	[illegible]	[illegible]	-	-	
Wexford,	[illegible]	[illegible]	[illegible]	-	[illegible]
Wicklow,	-	-	-	[illegible]	[illegible]
Total of Leinster,	[illegible]	[illegible]	[illegible]	[illegible]	[illegible]
Connaught:					
Galway,	[illegible]	[illegible]	-	-	[illegible]
Leitrim,	-	-	-	-	-
Mayo,	-	-	-	-	-
Roscommon,	-	-	-	-	[illegible]
Sligo,	-	-	-	-	-
Total of Connaught,	[illegible]	[illegible]	-	-	[illegible]
Munster:					
Clare,	-	-	-	-	-
Cork,	[illegible]	[illegible]	[illegible]	[illegible]	[illegible]
Kerry,	-	-	-	-	-
Limerick,	[illegible]	[illegible]	[illegible]	[illegible]	[illegible]
Tipperary,	-	[illegible]	-	-	[illegible]
Waterford,	-	-	-	-	-
Total of Munster,	[illegible]	[illegible]	[illegible]	[illegible]	[illegible]
Total of Ireland,	119	140	7	7	[illegible]

LXIX.—TABLE showing the Number of Applications by Leaseholders to the Land Commission to be declared Tenants of present tenancies (Form 61) during the three years ended 31st August, 1890.

Province and County.	Number of applications lodged.	Declared present Tenants.	Dismissed or struck out.	Withdrawn.	Number of applications pending.
ULSTER:					
Antrim,	[illegible]	[illegible]	-	-	[illegible]
Armagh,	[illegible]	[illegible]	-	-	-
Cavan,	[illegible]	[illegible]	-	[illegible]	-
Donegal,	-	-	-	-	-
Down,	[illegible]	[illegible]	-	[illegible]	-
Fermanagh,	[illegible]	-	-	-	[illegible]
Londonderry,	[illegible]	[illegible]	[illegible]	[illegible]	[illegible]
Monaghan,	[illegible]	[illegible]	-	-	-
Tyrone,	[illegible]	[illegible]	-	-	[illegible]
Total of Ulster,	[illegible]	[illegible]	[illegible]	[illegible]	[illegible]
LEINSTER:					
Carlow,	[illegible]	[illegible]	[illegible]	-	[illegible]
Dublin,	[illegible]	[illegible]	[illegible]	[illegible]	-
Kildare,	[illegible]	[illegible]	-	-	-
Kilkenny,	[illegible]	[illegible]	-	-	[illegible]
King's,	[illegible]	[illegible]	-	-	-
Longford,	[illegible]	[illegible]	-	-	[illegible]
Louth,	[illegible]	[illegible]	-	-	-
Meath,	[illegible]	[illegible]	-	-	[illegible]
Queen's,	[illegible]	[illegible]	-	-	[illegible]
Westmeath,	[illegible]	[illegible]	-	-	-
Wexford,	[illegible]	[illegible]	[illegible]	[illegible]	[illegible]
Wicklow,	[illegible]	[illegible]	-	[illegible]	[illegible]
Total of Leinster,	[illegible]	[illegible]	[illegible]	[illegible]	[illegible]
CONNAUGHT:					
Galway,	[illegible]	[illegible]	-	-	[illegible]
Leitrim,	[illegible]	[illegible]	-	-	-
Mayo,	[illegible]	[illegible]	-	-	-
Roscommon,	[illegible]	[illegible]	-	-	[illegible]
Sligo,	-	-	-	-	-
Total of Connaught,	[illegible]	[illegible]	-	-	[illegible]
MUNSTER:					
Clare,	-	-	-		
Cork,	[illegible]	[illegible]	[illegible]	[illegible]	[illegible]
Kerry,	[illegible]	[illegible]	-	-	-
Limerick,	[illegible]	[illegible]	[illegible]	[illegible]	[illegible]
Tipperary,	[illegible]	[illegible]	-	-	[illegible]
Waterford,	[illegible]	[illegible]	-	-	-
Total of Munster,	[illegible]	[illegible]	[illegible]	[illegible]	[illegible]
TOTAL OF IRELAND,	[illegible]	[illegible]	[illegible]	[illegible]	[illegible]

LXX.—TABLE showing the Number of Applications by Leaseholders to the Civil Bill Courts to be declared Tenants of present Tenancies (Form 61), during the year ended 31st August, 1890.

Province and County.	Number of applications lodged.	Declared present Tenants.	Dismissed or struck out.	Withdrawn.	Number of Applications pending.
MUNSTER:					
Cork,	-	-	-	-	[illegible]
Total,	-	-	-	-	[illegible]

LXXI.—TABLE showing the Number of Applications by Leaseholders to the Civil Bill Courts to be declared Tenants of present Tenancies (Form 81), during the three years ended 31st August, 1890.

PROVINCE AND COUNTY.	Number of applications received.	Declared present Tenants.	Dismissed or struck out.	Withdrawn.	Number of applications pending.
CONNAUGHT:					
Mayo,	1		1		
MUNSTER:					
Cork,	1	—	—	—	1
Total,	[illegible]	—	1	—	1
SUMMARY.					
Connaught,	[illegible]	—	1	—	[illegible]
Munster,	[illegible]	—	[illegible]	—	[illegible]
TOTAL,	[illegible]	—	1	—	[illegible]

SURRENDER OF HOLDINGS BY MIDDLEMEN.

Land Law (Ireland) Act, 1887, Sec. 3.

TABLES LXXII. to LXXV., inclusive.

LXXII.—TABLE showing the Number of Applications by Middlemen to the Land Commission, claiming to be entitled to surrender his Holding (Form 85), during the year ended the 21st August, 1890.

PROVINCE AND COUNTY.	Number of Applications received.	Number of applications transferred from Civil Bill Courts	Total.	Applications granted.	Applications dismissed or struck out.	Applications withdrawn.	Number of applications pending.
ULSTER:							
Armagh,	[illegible]	—	[illegible]	—	—	—	[illegible]
Total of Ulster,	[illegible]	—	[illegible]	—	—	—	[illegible]
LEINSTER:							
Kilkenny,	—	—	[illegible]	—	—	—	[illegible]
Total of Leinster,	—	[illegible]	[illegible]	—	—	—	[illegible]
CONNAUGHT:							
Galway,	[illegible]	—	[illegible]	—	—	1	—
Mayo,	—	—	—	—	[illegible]	—	[illegible]
Total of Connaught,	[illegible]	—	[illegible]	—	[illegible]	[illegible]	[illegible]
MUNSTER:							
Clare,	—	[illegible]	[illegible]	—	[illegible]	—	[illegible]
Waterford,	—	—	—	—	—	—	[illegible]
Total of Munster,	—	[illegible]	[illegible]	—	[illegible]	—	[illegible]
TOTAL OF IRELAND,	[illegible]	[illegible]	[illegible]	—	[illegible]	1	[illegible]

LXXIV.—TABLE showing the Number of Applications by Middleman to the Civil Bill Courts claiming to be entitled to surrender his Holding (Form 53), during the year ended the 31st August, 1890.

PROVINCE AND COUNTY.	Number of Applications lodged.	Number of Applications transferred from Civil Bill Courts.	Applications granted.	Applications dismissed or struck out.	Applications withdrawn.	Number of Applications pending.
LEINSTER:						
Kildare,	[illegible]	[illegible]	[illegible]	[illegible]	[illegible]	
King's,	[illegible]	[illegible]	[illegible]	[illegible]	[illegible]	
Queen's,	[illegible]	[illegible]	[illegible]	[illegible]	[illegible]	
Wicklow,	[illegible]	[illegible]	[illegible]	[illegible]	[illegible]	[illegible]
Total of Leinster,	[illegible]	[illegible]	[illegible]	[illegible]	[illegible]	[illegible]
MUNSTER:						
Cork,	[illegible]	[illegible]	[illegible]	[illegible]	...	[illegible]
Waterford,	[illegible]	[illegible]	[illegible]	[illegible]	...	[illegible]
Total of Munster,	[illegible]	[illegible]	[illegible]	[illegible]	[illegible]	[illegible]
TOTAL OF IRELAND,	[illegible]	[illegible]	[illegible]	[illegible]	[illegible]	[illegible]

LXXV.—TABLE showing the Number of Applications by Middleman to the Civil Bill Courts claiming to be entitled to surrender his Holding (Form 53), during the three years ended the 31st August, 1890.

PROVINCE AND COUNTY.	Number of Applications lodged.	Number of Applications transferred from Civil Bill Courts.	Applications granted.	Applications dismissed or struck out.	Applications withdrawn.	Number of Applications pending.
ULSTER:						
Armagh,	[illegible]	[illegible]	[illegible]	[illegible]	...	
Total of Ulster,	[illegible]	...	[illegible]	[illegible]	[illegible]	[illegible]
LEINSTER:						
Kildare,	[illegible]	[illegible]	[illegible]	[illegible]	[illegible]	[illegible]
King's,	[illegible]	[illegible]	[illegible]	[illegible]	[illegible]	[illegible]
Queen's,	[illegible]	[illegible]	[illegible]	[illegible]	[illegible]	[illegible]
Wicklow,	[illegible]	[illegible]	[illegible]	[illegible]	[illegible]	[illegible]
Total of Leinster,	[illegible]	[illegible]	[illegible]	[illegible]	[illegible]	[illegible]
CONNAUGHT:						
Mayo,	[illegible]	[illegible]	[illegible]	[illegible]	[illegible]	[illegible]
Total of Connaught,	[illegible]	[illegible]	[illegible]	[illegible]	[illegible]	[illegible]
MUNSTER:						
Cork,	[illegible]	[illegible]	[illegible]	[illegible]	[illegible]	
Limerick,	[illegible]	[illegible]	[illegible]	[illegible]	[illegible]	
Waterford,	[illegible]	[illegible]	[illegible]	[illegible]	[illegible]	[illegible]
Total of Munster,	[illegible]	[illegible]	[illegible]	[illegible]	...	[illegible]
TOTAL OF IRELAND,	[illegible]	[illegible]	[illegible]	[illegible]	[illegible]	[illegible]

LXXVI.—Proceedings of the Church Property and General Collection Branch, 44 & 45 Victoria, Chap. 72.

1. Annuities outstanding on 31st August, 1890.

Head of Account.	No.	Amount.		
		£	s.	d.
Incumbents,	12	3,465	4	10
Curates,	7	745	0	0
Vicars General,	5	348	10	0
Clerks, Sextons, &c.,	149	1,327	4	0
Nonconformist Ministers,	6	419	0	0
Assistants, 44th Section,	8	274	16	0
Total,	187	7,169	10	4

2. Sales of Property.

Head of Account.	No. of Lots sold.	Annual Rent or Value.			Purchase Money.		
		£	s.	d.	£	s.	d.
Perpetuity Rents,	8	655	18	3	16,334	7	6
Tithe Rentcharge for Cash,	136	1,011	14	11	22,356	15	8
Do. on Loan,	87	495	5	8	10,745	19	0

3. Collection of Revenue and Purchase Money.

——	Received in Cash.			Secured by Mortgage.		
	£	s.	d.	£	s.	d.
Purchase Money,	57,691	3	4	10,745	19	0
Revenue, &c.,	703,177	3	4	—		
Total Receipts,	760,868	6	8	10,745	19	0

Arrears of Revenue at 31st March, 1890, . . . £961,208 15s. 3d.

4. Discharge of Liabilities.

Commissioners for Reduction of National Debt, . . . £634,025 8s. 6d.

Arrears of Rent Act, 45 & 46 Victoria, Chap. 47.

LXXVII.—Proceedings from the 22nd August, 1889, to the 22nd August, 1890, under the Arrears of Rent (Ireland) Act, 1882.

Section 1, sub-section 1.

Amount paid.	Amount remaining unpaid.	Number of cases in which payment has not yet been made.
£ s. d.	£ s. d.	
4 15 3	3,787 15 11	508

Section 1, sub-section b.

Amount paid.	Amount remaining unpaid.	Number of cases in which payment has not yet been made.
£ s. d.	£ s. d.	
19 10 6	518 13 9	110

Section 16.

Amount settled.	Amount remaining unsettled.	Number of cases pending.
£ s. d.	£ s. d.	
Nil.	91 19 7	1

Section 17.

Nature of claim.	No. of cases.	Amount claimed to be refunded.	Amount of Rent certified to have been relinquished.
		£ s. d.	£ s. d.
Remission of Tithe Rent-charge, .	Nil.	Nil.	Nil.
" Income Tax, . .	Nil.	Nil.	Nil.
" Quit Rent, . .	Nil.	Nil.	Nil.

LXXVIII.—Collection of Agricultural Prices.—Yearly Returns.

Return of Average Prices of Agricultural Produce collected by the Irish Land Commission for the Year ended 31st December, 18[illegible].

Produce.		Province of Leinster.	Munster.	Ulster.	Connaught.	Whole of Ireland.
Crops:—		s. d.	s. d.	s. d.	s. d.	s. d.
Wheat,	per cwt.,	[illegible]	[illegible]	[illegible]	[illegible]	[illegible]
Oats,	"	[illegible]	[illegible]	[illegible]	[illegible]	[illegible]
Barley,	"	[illegible]	[illegible]	[illegible]	[illegible]	[illegible]
Flax,	per stone,	[illegible]	—	[illegible]	—	[illegible]
Potatoes,	per cwt.,	[illegible]	[illegible]	[illegible]	[illegible]	[illegible]
Hay,	"	[illegible]	[illegible]	[illegible]	[illegible]	[illegible]
Butter,	"	[illegible]	[illegible]	[illegible]	[illegible]	[illegible]
Beef,	"	[illegible]	[illegible]	[illegible]	[illegible]	[illegible]
Mutton,	"	[illegible]	[illegible]	[illegible]	[illegible]	[illegible]
Pork (Fresh),	"	[illegible]	[illegible]	[illegible]	[illegible]	[illegible]
Wool,	per lb.,	[illegible]	[illegible]	—	[illegible]	[illegible]
Cattle:—		£ s. d.	£ s. d.	£ s. d.	£ s. d.	£ s. d.
1st Class—One year old,		[illegible]	[illegible]	[illegible]	[illegible]	[illegible]
" Two years old,		[illegible]	[illegible]	[illegible]	[illegible]	[illegible]
" Three years old,		[illegible]	[illegible]	[illegible]	[illegible]	[illegible]
" Springers,		[illegible]	[illegible]	[illegible]	[illegible]	[illegible]
2nd Class—One year old,		[illegible]	[illegible]	[illegible]	[illegible]	[illegible]
" Two years old,		[illegible]	[illegible]	[illegible]	[illegible]	[illegible]
" Three years old,		[illegible]	[illegible]	[illegible]	[illegible]	[illegible]
" Springers,		[illegible]	[illegible]	[illegible]	[illegible]	[illegible]
3rd Class—One year old,		[illegible]	[illegible]	[illegible]	[illegible]	[illegible]
" Two years old,		[illegible]	[illegible]	[illegible]	[illegible]	[illegible]
" Three years old,		[illegible]	[illegible]	[illegible]	[illegible]	[illegible]
" Springers,		[illegible]	[illegible]	[illegible]	[illegible]	[illegible]
Average Prices of the above Three Classes of Cattle:—						
One year old,		[illegible]	[illegible]	[illegible]	[illegible]	[illegible]
Two years old,		[illegible]	[illegible]	[illegible]	[illegible]	[illegible]
Three years old,		[illegible]	[illegible]	[illegible]	[illegible]	[illegible]
Springers,		[illegible]	[illegible]	[illegible]	[illegible]	[illegible]
Lambs:—		s. d.	s. d.	s. d.	s. d.	s. d.
1st, 2nd, and 3rd Classes together,		[illegible]	[illegible]	[illegible]	[illegible]	[illegible]

LXXVIII.—COLLECTION OF AGRICULTURAL PRICES—YEARLY RETURNS—continued.

RETURN of AVERAGE PRICES of AGRICULTURAL PRODUCE collected by the Irish Land Commission for the Year ended 31st December, 188[illegible].

Produce.		Province of Leinster	Province of Munster	Province of Ulster	Province of Connaught	Whole of Ireland
		s. d.	s. d.	s. d.	s. d.	s. d.
CROPS:—						
Wheat,	per cwt.,	[illegible]	[illegible]	[illegible]	[illegible]	[illegible]
Oats,	"	[illegible]	[illegible]	[illegible]	[illegible]	[illegible]
Barley,	"	[illegible]	[illegible]	[illegible]	[illegible]	[illegible]
Flax,	per stone,	[illegible]	—	[illegible]	—	[illegible]
Potatoes,	per cwt.,	[illegible]	[illegible]	[illegible]	[illegible]	[illegible]
Hay,	"	[illegible]	[illegible]	[illegible]	[illegible]	[illegible]
BUTTER,	"	[illegible]	[illegible]	[illegible]	[illegible]	[illegible]
BEEF,	"	[illegible]	[illegible]	[illegible]	—	[illegible]
MUTTON,	"	[illegible]	[illegible]	[illegible]	—	[illegible]
PORK ([illegible]),	"	[illegible]	[illegible]	[illegible]	[illegible]	[illegible]
WOOL,	per lb.,	[illegible]	[illegible]	[illegible]	[illegible]	[illegible]
		£ s. d.	£ s. d.	£ s. d.	£ s. d.	£ s. d.
CATTLE:—						
1st Class—One year old,		[illegible]	[illegible]	[illegible]	[illegible]	[illegible]
" Two years old,		[illegible]	[illegible]	[illegible]	[illegible]	[illegible]
" Three years old,		[illegible]	[illegible]	[illegible]	[illegible]	[illegible]
" Springers,		[illegible]	[illegible]	[illegible]	[illegible]	[illegible]
2nd Class—One year old,		[illegible]	[illegible]	[illegible]	[illegible]	[illegible]
" Two years old,		[illegible]	[illegible]	[illegible]	[illegible]	[illegible]
" Three years old,		[illegible]	[illegible]	[illegible]	[illegible]	[illegible]
" Springers,		[illegible]	[illegible]	[illegible]	[illegible]	[illegible]
3rd Class—One year old,		[illegible]	[illegible]	[illegible]	[illegible]	[illegible]
" Two years old,		[illegible]	[illegible]	[illegible]	[illegible]	[illegible]
" Three years old,		[illegible]	[illegible]	[illegible]	[illegible]	[illegible]
" Springers,		[illegible]	[illegible]	[illegible]	[illegible]	[illegible]
AVERAGE PRICES OF THE THREE CLASSES OF CATTLE:—						
One year old,		[illegible]	[illegible]	[illegible]	[illegible]	[illegible]
Two years old,		[illegible]	[illegible]	[illegible]	[illegible]	[illegible]
Three years old,		[illegible]	[illegible]	[illegible]	[illegible]	[illegible]
Springers,		[illegible]	[illegible]	[illegible]	[illegible]	[illegible]
		s. d.	s. d.	s. d.	s. d.	s. d.
LAMBS:—						
1st, 2nd, and 3rd Classes together,		[illegible]	[illegible]	[illegible]	[illegible]	[illegible]

LXXIX.—Collection of Agricultural Prices—Quarterly Returns

Return of Average Prices of Agricultural Produce collected by the Irish Land Commission for the Quarter ended 31st March, 18[illegible].

Produce.		Leinster.	Munster.	Ulster.	Connaught.	Whole of Ireland.
CROPS—		s. d.	s. d.	s. d.	s. d.	s. d.
Wheat,	per cwt.,	[illegible]	[illegible]	[illegible]	[illegible]	[illegible]
Oats,	"	[illegible]	[illegible]	[illegible]	[illegible]	[illegible]
Barley,	"	[illegible]	[illegible]	[illegible]	[illegible]	[illegible]
Flax,	per stone,	—	—	[illegible]	—	[illegible]
Potatoes	per cwt.,	[illegible]	[illegible]	[illegible]	[illegible]	[illegible]
Hay,	"	[illegible]	[illegible]	[illegible]	[illegible]	[illegible]
BUTTER,	"	[illegible]	[illegible]	[illegible]	[illegible]	[illegible]
BEEF,	"	[illegible]	[illegible]	[illegible]	—	[illegible]
MUTTON,	"	[illegible]	[illegible]	[illegible]	—	[illegible]
PORK (Fresh),	"	[illegible]	[illegible]	[illegible]	[illegible]	[illegible]
WOOL,	per lb.	[illegible]	[illegible]	—	—	[illegible]
CATTLE—		£ s. d.	£ s. d.	£ s. d.	£ s. d.	£ s. d.
1st Class—One year old,		[illegible]	[illegible]	[illegible]	[illegible]	[illegible]
" Two years old,		[illegible]	[illegible]	[illegible]	[illegible]	[illegible]
" Three years old,		[illegible]	[illegible]	—	[illegible]	[illegible]
" Springers,		[illegible]	[illegible]	[illegible]	[illegible]	[illegible]
2nd Class—One year old,		[illegible]	[illegible]	[illegible]	[illegible]	[illegible]
" Two years old,		[illegible]	[illegible]	[illegible]	[illegible]	[illegible]
" Three years old,		[illegible]	[illegible]	[illegible]	[illegible]	[illegible]
" Springers,		[illegible]	[illegible]	[illegible]	[illegible]	[illegible]
3rd Class—One year old,		[illegible]	[illegible]	[illegible]	[illegible]	[illegible]
" Two years old,		[illegible]	[illegible]	[illegible]	[illegible]	[illegible]
" Three years old,		[illegible]	[illegible]	[illegible]	[illegible]	[illegible]
" Springers,		[illegible]	[illegible]	[illegible]	[illegible]	[illegible]
AVERAGE PRICES OF THE THREE CLASSES OF CATTLE—						
One year old,		[illegible]	[illegible]	[illegible]	[illegible]	[illegible]
Two years old,		[illegible]	[illegible]	[illegible]	[illegible]	[illegible]
Three years old,		[illegible]	[illegible]	[illegible]	[illegible]	[illegible]
Springers,		[illegible]	[illegible]	[illegible]	[illegible]	[illegible]

Return of Average Prices of Agricultural Produce collected by the Irish Land Commission for the Quarter ended 30th June, 1880.

Produce.		Province of Leinster.	Munster.	Ulster.	Connaught.	Whole of Ireland.
		s. d.	s. d.	s. d.	s. d.	s. d.
Crops.—						
Wheat,	per cwt.	[illegible]	[illegible]	[illegible]	[illegible]	[illegible]
Oats,	"	[illegible]	[illegible]	[illegible]	[illegible]	[illegible]
Barley,	"	[illegible]	[illegible]	—	—	[illegible]
Flax,	per stone.	—	—	[illegible]	—	[illegible]
Potatoes,	per cwt.,	[illegible]	[illegible]	[illegible]	[illegible]	[illegible]
Hay,	"	[illegible]	[illegible]	[illegible]	[illegible]	[illegible]
Butter,	"	[illegible]	[illegible]	[illegible]	[illegible]	[illegible]
***Beef,**	"	[illegible]	[illegible]	[illegible]	—	[illegible]
***Mutton,**	"	[illegible]	[illegible]	[illegible]	—	[illegible]
Pork (Fresh),	"	[illegible]	[illegible]	[illegible]	[illegible]	[illegible]
Wool,	per lb.	[illegible]	[illegible]	[illegible]	[illegible]	[illegible]
		£ s. d.	£ s. d.	£ s. d.	£ s. d.	£ s. d.
Cattle.—						
1st Class—One year old,		[illegible]	[illegible]	[illegible]	[illegible]	[illegible]
" Two years old,		[illegible]	[illegible]	[illegible]	[illegible]	[illegible]
" Three years old,		[illegible]	[illegible]	[illegible]	[illegible]	[illegible]
" Springers,		[illegible]	[illegible]	[illegible]	[illegible]	[illegible]
2nd Class—One year old,		[illegible]	[illegible]	[illegible]	[illegible]	[illegible]
" Two years old,		[illegible]	[illegible]	[illegible]	[illegible]	[illegible]
" Three years old,		[illegible]	[illegible]	[illegible]	[illegible]	[illegible]
" Springers,		[illegible]	[illegible]	[illegible]	[illegible]	[illegible]
3rd Class—One year old,		[illegible]	[illegible]	[illegible]	[illegible]	[illegible]
" Two years old,		[illegible]	[illegible]	[illegible]	[illegible]	[illegible]
" Three years old,		[illegible]	[illegible]	[illegible]	[illegible]	[illegible]
" Springers,		[illegible]	[illegible]	[illegible]	[illegible]	[illegible]
		s. d.	s. d.	s. d.	s. d.	s. d.
***Sheep.—**						
Lambs,		[illegible]	[illegible]	[illegible]	[illegible]	[illegible]
Hoggets,		[illegible]	[illegible]	[illegible]	[illegible]	[illegible]
Two years old and over,		[illegible]	[illegible]	[illegible]	[illegible]	[illegible]

* The Prices for Beef, Mutton, and Sheep are the average of 1st, 2nd, and 3rd qualities.

LXXIX.—Collection of Agricultural Prices.—Quarterly Returns—*continued.*

Return of Average Prices of Agricultural Produce collected by the Irish Land Commissioners for the Quarter ended 30th September, 1890.

Produce.	Leinster.	Munster.	Ulster.	Connaught.	Whole of Ireland.
	s. d.	s. d.	s. d.	s. d.	s. d.
GRAIN:—					
Wheat, per cwt.,	[illegible]	[illegible]	[illegible]	—	[illegible]
Oats, "	[illegible]	[illegible]	[illegible]	[illegible]	[illegible]
Barley, "	[illegible]	[illegible]	[illegible]	[illegible]	[illegible]
Flax, per stone,	—	—	[illegible]	—	[illegible]
Potatoes, per cwt.,	[illegible]	[illegible]	[illegible]	[illegible]	[illegible]
Hay, "	[illegible]	[illegible]	[illegible]	[illegible]	[illegible]
BUTTER, "	[illegible]	[illegible]	[illegible]	[illegible]	[illegible]
*BEEF, "	[illegible]	—	[illegible]	—	[illegible]
*MUTTON, "	[illegible]	—	[illegible]	—	[illegible]
PORK (Fresh), "	[illegible]	[illegible]	[illegible]	—	[illegible]
WOOL, per lb.,	[illegible]	[illegible]	[illegible]	[illegible]	[illegible]
	£ s. d.	£ s. d.	£ s. d.	£ s. d.	£ s. d.
CATTLE:—					
1st Class—One year old,	[illegible]	[illegible]	[illegible]	[illegible]	[illegible]
" Two years old,	[illegible]	[illegible]	[illegible]	[illegible]	[illegible]
" Three years old,	[illegible]	[illegible]	[illegible]	[illegible]	[illegible]
" Springers,	[illegible]	[illegible]	[illegible]	[illegible]	[illegible]
2nd Class—One year old,	[illegible]	[illegible]	[illegible]	[illegible]	[illegible]
" Two years old,	[illegible]	[illegible]	[illegible]	[illegible]	[illegible]
" Three years old,	[illegible]	[illegible]	[illegible]	[illegible]	[illegible]
" Springers,	[illegible]	[illegible]	[illegible]	[illegible]	[illegible]
3rd Class—One year old,	[illegible]	[illegible]	[illegible]	[illegible]	[illegible]
" Two years old,	[illegible]	[illegible]	[illegible]	[illegible]	[illegible]
" Three years old,	[illegible]	[illegible]	[illegible]	[illegible]	[illegible]
" Springers,	[illegible]	[illegible]	[illegible]	[illegible]	[illegible]
	s. d.	s. d.	s. d.	s. d.	s. d.
*SHEEP:—					
Lambs,	[illegible]	[illegible]	[illegible]	[illegible]	[illegible]
Hoggets,	[illegible]	[illegible]	[illegible]	[illegible]	[illegible]
Two years old and over,	[illegible]	[illegible]	[illegible]	[illegible]	[illegible]

* The Prices for Beef, Mutton, and Sheep are the average of 1st, 2nd, and 3rd qualities.

† It has not been possible during this quarter to obtain returns of the prices of Sheep for a large portion of Ulster. The average prices for this province are therefore not [illegible].

LXXI.—Collection of Agricultural Prices—Weekly Returns.

Live Weight Returns for the Week ended 2nd October, 1890.

The following Returns are those of actual Sales made in the Markets referred to, the Stock being weighed either before or after Sale.

Dublin, 2nd October.

No. of Beasts.	Description.	Quality.	Average Price per Head.	Average Live Weight.	Average Price per Cwt.
	FAT CATTLE:—		£ s. d.	Cwt. qrs. lb.	£ s. d.
[illegible]	Heifers,	Prime,	[illegible]	[illegible]	[illegible]
[illegible]	Do.,	do.,	[illegible]	[illegible]	[illegible]
[illegible]	Do.,	do.,	[illegible]	[illegible]	[illegible]
[illegible]	Bullocks,	Good,	[illegible]	[illegible]	[illegible]
[illegible]	Heifers,	do.,	[illegible]	[illegible]	[illegible]
[illegible]	Do.,	do.,	[illegible]	[illegible]	[illegible]
[illegible]	Bullocks,	Fair,	[illegible]	[illegible]	[illegible]
[illegible]	Do.,	do.,	[illegible]	[illegible]	[illegible]
[illegible]	Do.,	do.,	[illegible]	[illegible]	[illegible]
[illegible]	Heavy Heifers,	do.,	[illegible]	[illegible]	[illegible]
[illegible]	Bullocks,	Middling,	[illegible]	[illegible]	[illegible]
[illegible]	Do.,	do.,	[illegible]	[illegible]	[illegible]
[illegible]	Heifers,	do.,	[illegible]	[illegible]	[illegible]
[illegible]	Cows,	Infr.,	[illegible]	[illegible]	[illegible]
	FAT SHEEP:—				
[illegible]	Wethers,	Prime,	[illegible]	[illegible]	[illegible]
10	Do.,	do.,	[illegible]	[illegible]	[illegible]
[illegible]	Do.,	Good,	[illegible]	[illegible]	[illegible]
[illegible]	Do.,	do.,	[illegible]	[illegible]	[illegible]
[illegible]	Do.,	do.,	[illegible]	[illegible]	[illegible]
[illegible]	Do.,	do.,	[illegible]	[illegible]	[illegible]
[illegible]	Ewes,	Fair,	[illegible]	[illegible]	[illegible]
[illegible]	Do.,	do.,	[illegible]	[illegible]	[illegible]

LXXX.—Collection of Agricultural Prices.—Weekly Returns—continued.

Belfast, 30th September.

No. of Animals.	Description.	Quality.	Average Price per Head.	Average Live Weight.	Average Price per Cwt.
	FAT CATTLE:—		£ s. d.	Cwt. qr. lbs.	£ s. d.
[illegible]	Heifers,	Prime,	[illegible]	[illegible]	[illegible]
[illegible]	Do.,	Good,	[illegible]	[illegible]	[illegible]
[illegible]	Bullocks,	Prime,	[illegible]	[illegible]	[illegible]
[illegible]	Do.,	Middling,	[illegible]	[illegible]	[illegible]
[illegible]	Cows,	Good,	[illegible]	[illegible]	[illegible]
[illegible]	Do.,	Middling,	[illegible]	[illegible]	[illegible]
[illegible]	Do.,	Inferior,	[illegible]	[illegible]	[illegible]
	FAT SHEEP:—				
[illegible]	Ewes,	Inferior,	[illegible]	[illegible]	[illegible]

Live Weight Returns for the Week ended 10th October, 1890.

Dublin, 9th October.

No. of Animals.	Description.	Quality.	Average Price per Head.	Average Live Weight.	Average Price per Cwt.
	FAT CATTLE:—				
[illegible]	Bullocks,	Prime,	[illegible]	[illegible]	[illegible]
[illegible]	Do.,	do.,	[illegible]	[illegible]	[illegible]
[illegible]	Do.,	do.,	[illegible]	[illegible]	[illegible]
[illegible]	Bullocks,	do.,	[illegible]	[illegible]	[illegible]
[illegible]	Do.,	do.,	[illegible]	[illegible]	[illegible]
[illegible]	Heifers,	do.,	[illegible]	[illegible]	[illegible]
[illegible]	Do.,	Good,	[illegible]	[illegible]	[illegible]
[illegible]	Bullocks,	do.,	[illegible]	[illegible]	[illegible]
[illegible]	Heifers,	Fair,	[illegible]	[illegible]	[illegible]
[illegible]	Bullocks,	do.,	[illegible]	[illegible]	[illegible]
[illegible]	Do.,	Rough,	[illegible]	[illegible]	[illegible]
[illegible]	Do.,	do.,	[illegible]	[illegible]	[illegible]
[illegible]	Cows,	Good,	[illegible]	[illegible]	[illegible]
	FAT SHEEP:—				
[illegible]	Hoggets,	Prime,	[illegible]	[illegible]	[illegible]
[illegible]	Do.,	do.,	[illegible]	[illegible]	[illegible]
[illegible]	Do.,	do.,	[illegible]	[illegible]	[illegible]
[illegible]	Do.,	do.,	[illegible]	[illegible]	[illegible]
[illegible]	Do.,	do.,	[illegible]	[illegible]	[illegible]
[illegible]	Ewes,	Good,	[illegible]	[illegible]	[illegible]
[illegible]	Do.,	do.,	[illegible]	[illegible]	[illegible]
[illegible]	Do.,	Fair,	[illegible]	[illegible]	[illegible]

Cork, 9th October.

No. of Animals.	Description.	Quality.	Average Price per Head.	Average Live Weight.	Average Price per Cwt.
	FAT CATTLE:—				
[illegible]	Heifers,	Good,	[illegible]	[illegible]	[illegible]
[illegible]	Bullocks,	do.,	[illegible]	[illegible]	[illegible]
[illegible]	Heifers,	Fair,	[illegible]	[illegible]	[illegible]
[illegible]	Cows,	Extra good,	[illegible]	[illegible]	[illegible]
[illegible]	Do.,	Good,	[illegible]	[illegible]	[illegible]
[illegible]	Do.,	Inferior,	[illegible]	[illegible]	[illegible]
[illegible]	Do.,	do.,	[illegible]	[illegible]	[illegible]
	FAT SHEEP:—				
[illegible]	Wethers,	Extra size,	[illegible]	[illegible]	[illegible]
[illegible]	Ewes,	Medium,	[illegible]	[illegible]	[illegible]
	STORE CATTLE:—				
[illegible]	Two-year-olds,	—	[illegible]	[illegible]	[illegible]

LXXX.—Collection of Agricultural Prices.—Weekly Returns—continued.

Belfast, 7th October.

No. of Animals.	Description.	Quality.	Average Price per Head.	Average Live Weight.	Average Price per Cwt.
	FAT CATTLE—		£ s. d.	Cwt. qr. lb.	£ s. d.
[illegible]	Bullocks,	Prime,	[illegible]	[illegible]	[illegible]
[illegible]	Do.,	Inferior,	[illegible]	[illegible]	[illegible]
[illegible]	Heifers,	Good,	[illegible]	[illegible]	[illegible]
[illegible]	Do.,	do.,	[illegible]	[illegible]	[illegible]
[illegible]	Cows,	Prime,	[illegible]	[illegible]	[illegible]
[illegible]	Do.,	Middling,	[illegible]	[illegible]	[illegible]
[illegible]	Do.,	Inferior,	[illegible]	[illegible]	[illegible]
	FAT SHEEP—				
[illegible]	Ewes,	Good,	[illegible]	[illegible]	[illegible]
[illegible]	Do.,	do.,	[illegible]	[illegible]	[illegible]
[illegible]	Do. [illegible]	Inferior,	[illegible]	[illegible]	[illegible]

[illegible] Sheep Fair, 7th October.

[illegible]	Wethers,	Good,	[illegible]	[illegible]	[illegible]
[illegible]	Ewes,	do.,	[illegible]	[illegible]	[illegible]
[illegible]	Wethers,	Middling,	[illegible]	[illegible]	[illegible]
[illegible]	Do.,	[illegible]	[illegible]	[illegible]	[illegible]
[illegible]	[illegible]	[illegible]	[illegible]	[illegible]	[illegible]
[illegible]	Wethers,	Good,	[illegible]	[illegible]	[illegible]

[illegible], October.

	STORE CATTLE—				
[illegible]	Yearlings,		[illegible]	[illegible]	[illegible]

[illegible], October.

	STORE CATTLE—				
[illegible]	Yearlings,	—	[illegible]	[illegible]	[illegible]
[illegible]	[illegible]	Prime,	[illegible]	[illegible]	[illegible]
[illegible]	Do.,	do.,	[illegible]	[illegible]	[illegible]
[illegible]	Do.,	do.,	[illegible]	[illegible]	[illegible]

Live Weight Returns for Week ended 17th October, [illegible].

Dublin, 16th October.

	FAT CATTLE—				
[illegible]	Bullocks,	Prime,	[illegible]	[illegible]	[illegible]
[illegible]	Do.,	do.,	[illegible]	[illegible]	[illegible]
[illegible]	Do.,	do.,	[illegible]	[illegible]	[illegible]
[illegible]	Do.,	Good,	[illegible]	[illegible]	[illegible]
[illegible]	Do.,	do.,	[illegible]	[illegible]	[illegible]
[illegible]	Do.,	do.,	[illegible]	[illegible]	[illegible]
[illegible]	Do.,	Middling,	[illegible]	[illegible]	[illegible]
[illegible]	Heifers,	Good,	[illegible]	[illegible]	[illegible]
[illegible]	Do.,	do.,	[illegible]	[illegible]	[illegible]
[illegible]	Do.,	Middling,	[illegible]	[illegible]	[illegible]
[illegible]	Do.,	Rough,	[illegible]	[illegible]	[illegible]
[illegible]	Do.,	do.,	[illegible]	[illegible]	[illegible]
[illegible]	Do.,	do.,	[illegible]	[illegible]	[illegible]
[illegible]	Do.,	Inferior,	[illegible]	[illegible]	[illegible]
[illegible]	Cows,	Good,	[illegible]	[illegible]	[illegible]

LXXX.—Collection of Agricultural Prices.—Weekly Returns—continued.

Dublin, 16th October—continued.

No. of Beasts	Description.	Quality.	Average Price per Head.	Average Live Weight.	Average Price per cwt.
			£ s. d.	Cwt. qr. lbs.	£ s. d.
	FAT SHEEP.—				
[illegible]	Hoggets,	Good,	[illegible]	[illegible]	[illegible]
[illegible]	Do.,	do.,	[illegible]	[illegible]	[illegible]
[illegible]	Wethers,	do.,	[illegible]	[illegible]	[illegible]
[illegible]	Do.,	do.,	[illegible]	[illegible]	[illegible]
[illegible]	Do.,	do.,	[illegible]	[illegible]	[illegible]
[illegible]	Do.,	do.,	[illegible]	[illegible]	[illegible]
[illegible]	Do.,	Fair,	[illegible]	[illegible]	[illegible]
[illegible]	Ewes,	Good,	[illegible]	[illegible]	[illegible]

Cork, 16th October.

No. of Beasts	Description.	Quality.	Average Price per Head.	Average Live Weight.	Average Price per cwt.
	FAT CATTLE.—				
[illegible]	Heifers,	Fair,	[illegible]	[illegible]	[illegible]
[illegible]	Do.,	do.,	[illegible]	[illegible]	[illegible]
[illegible]	Do.,	do.,	[illegible]	[illegible]	[illegible]
[illegible]	Bullocks,	Rough,	[illegible]	[illegible]	[illegible]
[illegible]	Cows,	Good,	[illegible]	[illegible]	[illegible]
[illegible]	Do.,	Inferior,	[illegible]	[illegible]	[illegible]
	FAT SHEEP.—				
[illegible]	[illegible]	[illegible]	[illegible]	[illegible]	[illegible]

Belfast, 14th October.

No. of Beasts	Description.	Quality.	Average Price per Head.	Average Live Weight.	Average Price per cwt.
	FAT CATTLE.—				
[illegible]	Bullocks,	Prime,	[illegible]	[illegible]	[illegible]
[illegible]	Do.,	Middling,	[illegible]	[illegible]	[illegible]
[illegible]	Heifers,	Good,	[illegible]	[illegible]	[illegible]
[illegible]	Do.,	do.,	[illegible]	[illegible]	[illegible]
[illegible]	Do.,	Inferior,	[illegible]	[illegible]	[illegible]
[illegible]	Cows,	Good,	[illegible]	[illegible]	[illegible]
[illegible]	Do.,	Middling,	[illegible]	[illegible]	[illegible]
[illegible]	Do.,	Inferior,	[illegible]	[illegible]	[illegible]
	FAT SHEEP.—				
[illegible]	Ewes,	Good,	[illegible]	[illegible]	[illegible]
[illegible]	Do.,	Inferior,	[illegible]	[illegible]	[illegible]

[illegible], [illegible] October.

No. of Beasts	Description.	Quality.	Average Price per Head.	Average Live Weight.	Average Price per cwt.
	FAT CATTLE.—				
[illegible]	[illegible]	[illegible]	[illegible]	[illegible]	[illegible]
[illegible]	[illegible]	[illegible]	[illegible]	[illegible]	[illegible]
[illegible]	[illegible]	Middling,	[illegible]	[illegible]	[illegible]
	STORE CATTLE.—				
[illegible]	[illegible] year-old [illegible]	Very good, [illegible]	[illegible]	[illegible]	[illegible]
[illegible]	Do.,	do.,	[illegible]	[illegible]	[illegible]
[illegible]	[illegible] year-old [illegible]	Well-bred, [illegible] quality,	[illegible]	[illegible]	[illegible]
	FAT SHEEP.—				
[illegible]	Hoggets,	Good, [illegible]	[illegible]	[illegible]	[illegible]
	STORE SHEEP.—				
[illegible]	Hoggets,	[illegible] quality,	[illegible]	[illegible]	[illegible]

LXXX.—Collection of Agricultural Prices.—Weekly Returns—*continued*.

Ballinasloe, 10th October.

No. of Beasts	Description.	Quality.	Average Price per Head	Average Live Weight	Average Price per Cwt.
			£ s. d.	Cwt. qr. lbs.	£ s. d.
	STORE CATTLE:—				
[illegible]	Heifers,	Good,	[illegible]	[illegible]	[illegible]
[illegible]	Bullocks,	do.,	[illegible]	[illegible]	[illegible]
[illegible]	Do.,	do.,	[illegible]	[illegible]	[illegible]
[illegible]	Do.,	Inferior,	[illegible]	[illegible]	[illegible]

Live Weight Returns for Week ended 24th October, 1890.

Dublin, 23rd October.

No. of Beasts	Description.	Quality.	Average Price per Head	Average Live Weight	Average Price per Cwt.
	FAT CATTLE:—				
[illegible]	Heifers,	Prime,	[illegible]	[illegible]	[illegible]
[illegible]	Do.,	do.,	[illegible]	[illegible]	[illegible]
[illegible]	Do.,	do.,	[illegible]	[illegible]	[illegible]
[illegible]	Do.,	do.,	[illegible]	[illegible]	[illegible]
[illegible]	Do.,	Good,	[illegible]	[illegible]	[illegible]
[illegible]	Do.,	Middling,	[illegible]	[illegible]	[illegible]
[illegible]	Do.,	Inferior,	[illegible]	[illegible]	[illegible]
[illegible]	Do.,	do.,	[illegible]	[illegible]	[illegible]
[illegible]	Bullocks,	Prime,	[illegible]	[illegible]	[illegible]
[illegible]	Do.,	Good,	[illegible]	[illegible]	[illegible]
[illegible]	Do.,	do.,	[illegible]	[illegible]	[illegible]
[illegible]	Do.,	do.,	[illegible]	[illegible]	[illegible]
[illegible]	Do.,	do.,	[illegible]	[illegible]	[illegible]
[illegible]	Do.,	do.,	[illegible]	[illegible]	[illegible]
	FAT SHEEP:—				
[illegible]	Wethers,	Prime,	[illegible]	[illegible]	[illegible]
[illegible]	Do.,	do.,	[illegible]	[illegible]	[illegible]
[illegible]	Hoggets,	do.,	[illegible]	[illegible]	[illegible]
[illegible]	Do.,	do.,	[illegible]	[illegible]	[illegible]
[illegible]	Do.,	Good,	[illegible]	[illegible]	[illegible]
[illegible]	Do.,	do.,	[illegible]	[illegible]	[illegible]
[illegible]	Ewes,	do.,	[illegible]	[illegible]	[illegible]

Belfast, 21st October.

No. of Beasts	Description.	Quality.	Average Price per Head	Average Live Weight	Average Price per Cwt.
	FAT CATTLE:—				
[illegible]	Heifers,	Prime,	[illegible]	[illegible]	[illegible]
[illegible]	Do.,	Good,	[illegible]	[illegible]	[illegible]
[illegible]	Do.,	Inferior,	[illegible]	[illegible]	[illegible]
[illegible]	Bullocks,	Prime,	[illegible]	[illegible]	[illegible]
[illegible]	Do.,	Good,	[illegible]	[illegible]	[illegible]
[illegible]	Do.,	Middling,	[illegible]	[illegible]	[illegible]
[illegible]	Do.,	Inferior,	[illegible]	[illegible]	[illegible]
[illegible]	Cows,	Good,	[illegible]	[illegible]	[illegible]
[illegible]	Do.,	Inferior,	[illegible]	[illegible]	[illegible]
	FAT SHEEP:—				
[illegible]	Ewes,	Fair,	[illegible]	[illegible]	[illegible]
[illegible]	Do.,	Inferior,	[illegible]	[illegible]	[illegible]

LXXI.—COLLECTION OF AGRICULTURAL PRICES.—WEEKLY RETURNS—*continued.*

CORK, 23rd OCTOBER.

No. of Return.	Description.	Quality.	Average Price per Head.	Average Live Weight.	Average Price per Cwt.
	FAT CATTLE—		£ s. d.	Cwt. qr. lb.	£ s. d.
[illegible]	Heifers,	Fair,	[illegible]	[illegible]	[illegible]
[illegible]	Do.,	do.,	[illegible]	[illegible]	[illegible]
[illegible]	Do.,	do.,	[illegible]	[illegible]	[illegible]
[illegible]	Cows,	Very good,	[illegible]	[illegible]	[illegible]
[illegible]	Do.,	Poor,	[illegible]	[illegible]	[illegible]
[illegible]	Do.,	Inferior,	[illegible]	[illegible]	[illegible]
[illegible]	Do.,	do.,	[illegible]	[illegible]	[illegible]
	FAT SHEEP—				
[illegible]	Sheep,	Prime,	[illegible]	[illegible]	[illegible]

TUAM.

	STORE CATTLE—				
	Three-year-old Bullocks,	Large,	[illegible]	[illegible]	
	Two-year-old Bullocks,	Good quality,	[illegible]	[illegible]	
	Two-and-a-half-year-old Heifers,	Good,	[illegible]	[illegible]	

Dublin Castle,

27th November, 1890.

SIR,

I have to acknowledge the receipt of your letter of this date, forwarding for submission to His Excellency the Lord Lieutenant, the Report of the Irish Land Commission for the year ended 31st August, 1890.

I am, Sir,

Your obedient Servant,

(Signed), WEST RIDGEWAY.

The Secretary,

Land Commission.

www.ingramcontent.com/pod-product-compliance
Lightning Source LLC
Chambersburg PA
CBHW021526270326
41930CB00008B/1106
9783741199882